THE KINGDOM OF THE MIND

INSCRIBED TO

FRANCES MANSBRIDGE

WHOSE UNTIRING DEVOTION
MADE THESE THINGS
POSSIBLE

ALBERT MANSBRIDGE

THE KINGDOM
OF THE MIND

Essays & Addresses
1903—37
of
Albert Mansbridge

SELECTED AND INTRODUCED
BY LEONARD CLARK

WITH A FOREWORD BY
G. M. TREVELYAN
Master of Trinity College
Cambridge

J. M. DENT & SONS LTD.

FOREWORD

Our debt to Albert Mansbridge is great. His work, methods, and personality are well though briefly described in the Introduction to this book by its compiler, Mr. Leonard Clark.

Early in life, by his native genius, unaided by university education or any other special advantages, it was given him to perceive that one of the greatest needs of our democratic society was humane education enjoyed by all classes, an education not stopping at the end of the school age, but going on throughout the life of men and women. Technical and scientific education are not enough. Good citizenship and the higher products of civilization both depend on the things of the spirit and imagination, which were in the greatest danger of being lost in a mechanical and material world. This danger is even greater than when Mansbridge started out on his astonishing campaign. But the danger would be greater still but for the remarkable degree of success that has attended his efforts.

G. M. Trevelyan

CONTENTS

		PAGE
FOREWORD. By G. M. Trevelyan		v
INTRODUCTION. By the Editor		ix

1. CO-OPERATION, TRADE UNIONISM, AND UNIVERSITY
   EXTENSION (1903)   1
   Three foundation articles of the Workers' Edu-
   cational Association.

2. WORKING MEN AND CONTINUATION SCHOOLS (1907)   12
   From *Continuation Schools in England and Else-*
   where, edited by Sir Michael Sadler.

3. UNIVERSITY TUTORIAL CLASSES (1912) . .   28
   An address at the Congress of Universities of the
   British Empire.

4. EDUCATION AND WORSHIP (1916) . . .   34
   No. 18 of Wartime Tracts for the Workers.

5. CHURCH TUTORIAL CLASSES (1917) . . .   38
   An article in the *Church Quarterly Review*.

6. CITIZENSHIP (1917)   45
   Chapter V of *Cambridge Essays on Education*,
   edited by A. C. Benson.

7. MEMBERS ONE OF ANOTHER (1918) . .   64
   Sermon preached in Salisbury Cathedral.

8. IDEALS AS FACTS (1923)   74
   From *The Way Out*, edited by the Rt. Hon.
   Oliver Stanley, M.P.

9. EXCEPT YE BECOME AS LITTLE CHILDREN (1926)   90
   A sermon preached in the Chapel of Trinity
   College, Cambridge.

PAGE

10. THE CITIZENSHIP OF THE TEACHER (1927) . 100
    Foundation oration at the London Day Training
    College.

11. THE WATERS OF LEARNING (1927) . . . 108
    Commencement address, University of Pitts-
    burgh, U.S.A.

12. THE POWER OF THE SPIRIT (1928) . . . 119
    Chapter I of *The Educated Life*.

13. AN INAUGURAL ADDRESS (1929) . . . 128
    Delivered at the World Conference on Adult
    Education.

14. THE DEDICATION OF LIFE (1930) . . . 143
    Second annual Haldane Memorial Lecture,
    Birkbeck College, University of London.

15. THE DYNAMIC OF LIFE (1932) 163
    Concluding address of the Conference of Works
    Directors at University College, Oxford.

16. THE DEMANDS OF THE ORDINARY MAN (1933) . 177
    From *Christianity and the Crisis*, edited by Dr.
    Percy Dearmer.

17. SOME WORKMAN SCHOLARS (1937) . . . 187
    Foundation oration, University of London In-
    stitute of Education.

ACKNOWLEDGMENTS AND LIST OF BOOKS BY ALBERT
    MANSBRIDGE 200

INTRODUCTION

I rise from the region of man, and soar to the border of God.—ALFRED WILLIAMS

HE who visits St. Paul's Cathedral looks around him in vain for a statue to its architect until he observes the inscription, 'Si monumentum requiris, circumspice.' The temple which rises in beauty by Thames side itself immortalizes its creator.

That which was carved in the cathedral stone about Christopher Wren can also be said of Albert Mansbridge, 'the architect of modern adult education,' as Professor Dover Wilson once wrote of him. The Workers' Educational Association, which he founded, will recall his name and be sufficient memorial to him for all time; and it was his privilege and rightful reward to see it develop, before his compulsory retirement from it due to stricken health in 1915, to an unchallenged position as a world-wide establishment.

Throughout his life Albert Mansbridge has preached the doctrine of higher non-vocational education for working men and women, whatever their trade, business, or profession. His unabated efforts have succeeded in bringing true scholarship into direct line with daily life, so that at the present time his doctrine has to a large extent permeated the national consciousness and is accepted as a natural constituent of our social system.

It is significant to learn that he had his beginnings in that class of working people to whose spiritual interests the whole of his life has been dedicated. From his earliest years he saw and knew the need of a liberal education for all men, and it is by reason of his first-hand knowledge of the unexpressed desires of his fellows, coupled with his personal integrity, that he has been enabled in large measure to satisfy these desires.

Albert Mansbridge was born in Gloucester in 1876. His parents were whole-hearted supporters of the ideals which are the authentic basis of the Co-operative movement. His mother was one of the first members and always an active participant of the Women's Co-operative Guild. She had wide sympathies and a balanced attitude to the problems of everyday life. The atmosphere of their simple home was one where a love of learning for itself and unselfish service to the community flowered naturally and soberly. The training given in self-dependence and high standards of personal conduct was a product of delicate and far-seeing minds.

Albert Mansbridge may be described as a typical Anglo-Saxon. He stands some six feet high, broad-shouldered, with a shock of fair hair, now whitening, ruddy of complexion as are the yeomen from whose stock he sprang. He has a habit of fixing those with whom he converses with eyes that are intensely blue and vivid, exploring as it would seem the inmost recesses of their minds. Those eyes deny the withholding of secrets, even as his forthright speech exposes his own sincerity and the truth in him. He can be blunt in argument, but usually he propounds his ideas in so evocative and stimulating a manner that, if his interviewer possesses only a spark of original perception, its fires will be produced. The fertility of Mansbridge's mind is to be seen in monuments such as the W.E.A., the National Central Library, the Seafarers' Education Service with the College of the Sea, and as our educational system develops his influence will make its impress with ever greater depth.

His powers of persuasiveness are not those employed by the skilful and eloquent advocate. It has been the righteousness of the causes he has espoused which has given his voice and pen their strength of attraction and conviction. Not only has he achieved things himself, often in the face of discouragement and prejudice, but he has succeeded in persuading men of all degrees to work with him and for his ideas. Among his supporters have been Cabinet ministers, bishops, the heads of universities and colleges, business magnates, and educational authorities and experts of all kinds. A generous man of great wealth, who supported Albert

Mansbridge with a blank cheque on more than one occasion, recently said of him: 'He is the most dangerous man in England. He taught the working people to think for themselves.' That was said with dry good humour, but no greater compliment could have been paid to Albert Mansbridge. Probably those whom he has benefited most know least about him, for he has always eschewed publicity.

His early schooling was received at a dame school in Gloucester, which he remembers affectionately as 'Old Mother Musty's,' and at St. James's national school, which was near by. But before his fifth birthday he was on the roll of Jessop Road infants' school, Herne Hill, for the Mansbridges had moved from the west country to London. Further schooling followed at Bolingbroke Road infants' school, Battersea, and, until he was nearly ten years old, at the Surrey Lane board school. It was from this latter that he gained a scholarship to Sir Walter St. John's middle school, and then to Battersea grammar school, where he remained until he was just fourteen years old. Then he left to earn his living as an office boy in the City.

Thus precipitated into business life, for the next few years he left home each day at 7.45 a.m. to return to it each evening at 7.15 p.m. It became his daily habit to walk from Battersea to the office where he was employed, a distance of some five miles, whereby he not only saved his twopenny fare, but was afforded the opportunity of thinking and dreaming more effectively. Then began a determined quest for knowledge. He was inspired by the programme of studies offered by University Extension, attended evening classes, and received some simple introductions to Latin, Greek, chemistry, and political economy. He began to discover other regions in the kingdom of the mind.

Aided to some extent by these spare-time studies Albert Mansbridge left his City office and passed into one of the lower grades of the civil service, first as a boy copyist in the Board of Inland Revenue at Somerset House, and then as a boy clerk in the office of the Committee of the Privy Council on Education—later to become the Board of Education.

The move 'up west' to Whitehall is an early landmark in his career, for he discovered Westminster Abbey, which, as Mr. J. L. Paton has so aptly said, 'became his university.' In the abbey he was able to sit at the feet of the Gamaliels of the day. He soon found himself profoundly moved and influenced by the rhetoric and doctrine of those brilliant divines and preachers who graced the Anglican pulpits during the later Victorian years.

It was now that Albert Mansbridge became the editor of an unofficial civil service magazine, *The Union Observer*, which he had founded shortly after his translation to Whitehall. Boldly daring, he invited Canon Gore, whom he had heard preach at the abbey, to contribute to one of the earlier numbers. The request was unsuccessful in spite of its forthrightness, but Gore was interested sufficiently to invite the young man to meet him in Little Cloisters. That meeting was a momentous one, for Gore became a friend for life, and his personal influence and warm sympathies during those impressionable, burning years were paramount for Albert Mansbridge. In Gore's home he met many notable people, and greatly enlarged his experience, widening his vision and extending his knowledge of men and the problems of life which they encountered daily.

Before he was twenty-one Albert Mansbridge had left the civil service and had become a clerk at the tea desk of the Co-operative Wholesale Society in Whitechapel. The return to 'the east' brought fresh experiences and different problems, but he became even more convinced that the educational needs of ordinary men and women were not being satisfied. It may well be that memories of his warehouse life originated a desire which led him, many years later, to set up and operate the Seafarers' Education Service. This service has revolutionized the supplying of books to seamen, and provides comprehensive educational facilities for man, woman, and boy serving in ships; it called forth from the late Duke of Kent the tribute that it was 'a university of the sea with many fine graduates.'

Albert Mansbridge remained 'in tea' for five years. Then

he joined the staff of the Co-operative Permanent Building Society, of which he is now the president. In 1900 he married Frances Pringle, the daughter of John Pringle of Dublin, and he had chosen well, for she brought to the partnership great foresight and steadfastness which, coupled with his own enthusiasm and energy, always brought his ships safely and proudly home. It is impossible to think of his wide range of public work without remembering Frances Mansbridge's close co-operation and personal sacrifices.

About the time of his marriage the clerk had the opportunity to try his hand at teaching. The first classes he taught were in industrial history, and his students mainly keen co-operative employees. Results were so outstandingly successful that he was appointed to teach economics and industrial history in the evening higher commercial schools of the London Board. For several years his classes at Sherbrooke Road evening school, Fulham, were considered to be some of the most efficient and original in the London area; and this at a period when he was working nine hours daily at his desk, leaving home at 7.30 a.m. and returning at 11 p.m.

His development was natural and unhurried. His background and daily contacts were the right soil for what was to germinate in him—the idea of fusing the ideals of the Co-operative and Trade Union movements with those of the universities. The result was to be the boldest experiment in working-class education since the 1870 Education Act.

In 1898 Albert Mansbridge had attended, as the result of an examination success, the Co-operative Congress at Peterborough, where he delivered so remarkable and outspoken a speech that it gained for him the friendship of Michael Sadler and Hudson Shaw, and an invitation to speak during the University Extension summer meeting at Oxford in the following August. He seized this chance with both hands, and choosing as his subject 'The Education of the Citizen,' he boldly advocated direct alliance between University Extension and the Co-operative movement. The Workers' Educational Association was thus born, and in 1903 he became its first and unpaid secretary—appointed by Frances Mansbridge, its first member.

The new association had reached such proportions by 1905 that it was evident it would require his full-time energies. So he resigned from the building society. This decision was indeed the parting of the ways for him; but, with the full and active support of his wife, he relinquished a reasonably well-paid and safe position for the hard and uncertain task of developing adult education in England, and with very limited pecuniary resources. The fire and faith within him could not be quenched or dimmed, and as the Workers' Educational Association grew in strength of numbers and purpose from year to year, so he grew in spiritual stature, and took men with him.

Now began the period of establishing the machinery necessary for bringing his philosophy into actual practice. Each year he extended his scope, working to a well-thought-out plan of action, and with his eyes on the future. In 1906 he became a member of the Consultative Committee of the Board of Education; in 1908 he founded the Central Joint Advisory Committee on University Tutorial Classes. An address delivered in London at the first Congress of Universities of the Empire in 1912 brought an invitation to visit the universities and Labour organizations of Australia. His acceptance of this was only made possible by Joseph Rowntree enabling the Workers' Educational Association to be carried on during his absence from England, and by Sir James Barrett, through the University of Melbourne, bearing the costs of the journey for himself and his wife. After almost uninterrupted lecturing and organizing during the autumn and winter of 1913 and the early spring of 1914, Albert Mansbridge left behind him branches of the Workers' Educational Association functioning in every Australian state. On the return journey to England he initiated the work in New Zealand and Canada. He had brought the universities to the doorsteps of the workers of the empire.

Dr. Lang, when Archbishop of Canterbury, speaking once on religious adult education, referred to Albert Mansbridge as 'the father of us all,' and on another occasion said: 'The prophet, let us recall, was Albert Mansbridge.' His successor in the archbishopric, Dr. William Temple, wrote in 1915: 'Our country and the future democracy are his debtors.' On arriving back in England Albert Mansbridge became occupied in a new field. Remembering the earlier teaching of Charles Gore, and believing that educational training must be complementary to the life of the spirit, he served, between 1914 and 1916, on a number of important church committees. Again and again he stressed the need for well-organized and informative adult religious education from which would automatically spring the richness of inner revelation as well as material knowledge.

In 1914, whilst actually sitting on the Selborne Committee on Church and State, Albert Mansbridge was suddenly struck down by the then little known but deadly cerebro-spinal meningitis. All work had to cease, and for weeks he hovered between life and death. That he eventually recovered was due in large measure to the devotion and skill of Dr. W. E. Gye, who, although a young man, diagnosed the disease correctly; he has since become a world authority on cancer. The late Sir Henry Head, whom Gye called in, stated that this recovery was the greatest medical miracle he had experienced in his career. A full return to normal health was, however, necessarily slow. A dozen years of strain and concentrated effort had seriously sapped his vitality, and acting upon the wise advice of his friends and colleagues in 1915, Albert Mansbridge resigned from the secretaryship of the Workers' Educational Association.

At this point in Mansbridge's career his activities, almost always in the field of modern adult education, become so manifold that there is not space to deal with them adequately and by connected narrative in a brief survey of this kind. Some record, however, of the main achievements and events of the next twenty-five years of his life must find a place here, and the following bald chronological summary is therefore offered with apologies to Dr. Mansbridge and to the reader.

1915–18: member of the Prime Minister's Committee on the teaching of Modern Languages. 1916: founded the Central Library for Students, and was its chairman until its incorporation by Royal Charter in 1931 as the National Central Library, when he became chairman of the trustees. 1917: member of the Adult Education Committee of the Ministry of Reconstruction. 1918–19: expert adviser to the British and Australian Army Education Services, and lecturer to the special schools at Cambridge for Australian and at Oxford for English officers. 1918: founded the World Association for Adult Education, and was its chairman until 1929, when he became its president in succession to President Masaryk of Czechoslovakia. 1919–22: member of the Royal Commission on the Universities of Oxford and Cambridge. 1919: founded the Seafarers' Education Service; appointed lecturer in civics at Cuddesdon Theological College, Oxford, which office he still holds. 1921: founded, with the co-operation of Lord Haldane, the British Institute of Adult Education. 1922–6: member of the Statutory Commission on the University of Oxford. 1922: lecturer on the Lowell Foundation, Boston, U.S.A., and again in 1934; appointed a life trustee of Shakespeare's Birthplace, Stratford-on-Avon. 1924–7: member of the Board of Education Departmental Committee on Public Libraries. 1924: member of the Adult Education Committee of the Board of Education, and later its vice-chairman. 1925: appointed to the staff of the Gilchrist Trustees to deliver lectures on 'The Story of Oxford and Cambridge.' 1926: delivered course of Earle Lectures in connection with the University of California and the Pacific School of Religion. 1927: reappointed member of the Consultative Committee of the Board of Education; orator at Commencement, University of Pittsburgh, U.S.A. 1930: toured Newfoundland and created its Adult Education Association. 1936: invited by the Association of American Colleges to deliver inaugural and other lectures. 1937: vice-chairman, Rachael McMillan Training College; chairman, Abbotsholme School, Derbyshire. 1938: invited by the Canadian Education Association to deliver annual address and to visit universities in the Maritime Provinces; honorary director of the College of the Sea, founded as a department of the Seafarers' Education Service. 1939: initiated Sea War Library Service on basis of the Seafarers' Education Service and British Ship Adoption Society.

Albert Mansbridge holds honorary degrees from the Universities of Oxford, Cambridge, Manchester, Pittsburgh, and Mount Allison, Canada. He is a member of the Council of Selwyn College, Cambridge, was for many years a governor of St. Hilda's College, Oxford, of St. Olave's Grammar School, Southwark (appointed by the University of Cambridge), and the Frances Mary Buss School (appointed by the University of Oxford). He is a member of Trinity College, Cambridge, and of Hertford College, Oxford, and chairman of the Thomas Wall Educational Trust. In 1931 the Order of the Companions of Honour was conferred upon him by H.M. King George V.

From this recital of work done and of the recognition given to that work, it is to be seen that, in the words of Professor J. H. Jones, of Leeds University, Albert Mansbridge has been enabled 'to achieve the biggest educational revolution of his generation.' He planted the seed of promise when he founded the Workers' Educational Association at the beginning of the century; he personally carried that seed and its living gospel to other countries, and left it to germinate in willing soil. But the Workers' Educational Association was only one part of the vision; the other was to provide the right *kind* of adult education in conjunction with the Universities. Mansbridge saw that the right kind of adult education was impossible without proper access to books; the Universities had always known that a well-stocked library must be the focal point of all adult education. So, in 1916, there followed as part of the whole pattern, the Central Library for Students, now the great National Central Library, which draws upon 21,000,000 books.

The World Association for Adult Education and the

British Institute for Adult Education are boughs of the main stem, and meanwhile a new branch was brought into being with the inauguration of the Seafarers' Education Service in 1919, which blossomed into the College of the Sea in 1938. All have grown concentrically around and in rhythm with the purposeful personality of Albert Mansbridge, who at no time sought to gather a premature harvest, or to administer established organizations, but who aimed rather at creating new means to an all-embracing end.

It is natural that a considerable body of scattered but important writings by him, published and unpublished, should have accumulated. Many of his friends, both in the British Empire and the United States, have felt that the time has arrived when a collection of this material should be made, so that it can be preserved in accessible and permanent form. It has been my privilege to carry out this task. The selection has meant reading through most of what he has written since 1903, and choosing from this vast storehouse. It is hardly necessary to say that without the co-operation of Albert Mansbridge no selection could have been made. It has never been easy to get information out of him, for he is a modest and retiring man, but when he realized what was involved, and saw that his friends were adamant, he capitulated and produced all the documents which he thought might be of use. In making the choices—entirely personal ones—I have borne in mind that they should present both a valuable piece of contemporary educational history and essential material for Albert Mansbridge's future biographers. For these addresses and articles deal with the genesis and development of most aspects of modern continuative education, and as such have been deliberately arranged in chronological order. This book, then, may be considered particularly opportune at a time when men and women are so deeply concerned with educational changes through new legislation.

Albert Mansbridge remains active. This Englishman, with his warm heart and breezy good humour, his capacity to make and keep friends, his energy and his ability to make quick decisions, moves as he did forty years ago, 'through the power of the spirit, through knowledge and training, to order the material of the world for the welfare of men and the glory of God.'

LEONARD CLARK

1. CO-OPERATION, TRADE UNIONISM, AND UNIVERSITY EXTENSION

(These three articles are reprints from the *University Extension Journal*, and the foundation of the Workers' Educational Association was inspired by and based on them. The first article, 'The Veneer,' published in January 1903, suggests that University Extension, allied with trade unionism and co-operation, will lead to true citizenship. In the second article, 'A Plan of Action,' published in March 1903, definite plans are advanced as to how the various democratic movements can proceed to develop higher education in co-operation with University Extension, as outlined in the January article. In 'An Association,' published in May 1903, a pioneer Association is devised which will attempt to forge a link between the democratic movements and University Extension. The Workers' Educational Association was founded in 1903.)

I. The Veneer

IT is probably true, as was recently remarked in a well-known weekly paper—that 'there never has been a time when everything offered to the public needed more searching examination than at the present'—which state of affairs undoubtedly indicates superficiality in the public mind. Superficiality is often resultant upon the misuse of knowledge acquired in the first stage of education. It is certain that the essential knowledge of the 'three R's' operates as a double-edged tool. Whilst it opens up the beautiful and true, it also opens up the cheap and changing opinions of a tuned press, which it itself creates.

To put it in another way: Democracy is suffering from a hard veneer, which elementary education, misused, has laid upon it. True education directly induces thought, which permeates the whole of society, and is the direct opposite of veneer. An education which merely promotes an unthinking absorption of facts, however numerous, places men more at the mercy of the opinion of the hour, however irresponsible, and renders them more susceptible to flights of mere rhetoric. Democracy is in this parlous condition. The veneer is upon it—a veneer which looks wise but makes no real contribution to the common thought; which induces tasks too great for its narrow capacity; which encourages fools and retards angels. .

Working men to-day are all afire to act politically. Their Mecca is Parliament, their local temple the municipality. The plank of their platform is Labour representation: a state of affairs highly to be desired, if it be the result of normal evolution preconditioned by wise education, but at present it bears no such evidence. If it be admitted, reasonably enough, that working men, as they stand, should be represented on governing bodies, it must also be admitted that lack of thinking power in the rank and file tends to nullify the good effect of such representation, however capable the representatives themselves.

The operation of wise and free education upon democracy would cause it to be an organic, contemplative, and expressive whole; its individual members sustained and controlled by the spirit of the whole body, its leaders in the van. Co-operation and trade unionism are the chief movements of democracy. University Extension, of all educational movements, promises most to be capable of infusing them with a wise and free education.

The appeal of the hour to trade unionists and co-operators is that they make political strokes, promote Bills, register protests, and send deputations to responsible ministers. The true appeal is that they lift themselves up through higher knowledge to higher works and higher pleasures, which, if responded to, will inevitably bring about right and sound action upon municipal, national, and imperial affairs; action brought about without conscious effort—the only effectual action. It will be promoted by wise and free education and sustained by it. That is my interpretation of the message of University Extension to the two great movements of democracy. The crux of the whole matter is this. If it be that the working man has been so induced to live as to find difficulty, conscious or unconscious, in making his own contribution of thought to the common life, whether it be the fault of an educational system, as such, or no, a wise and forceful educational corrective is necessary; and University Extension undoubtedly supplies that corrective.

In the past University Extension has not allied itself with trade unionism as such, but it has done so with co-operation. Trade unionists and co-operators are, however, evincing a tendency to recognize unity of interests, and it will be impossible for friends of education who look forward into the future to consider the two movements apart. Co-operators have realized in some measure the glory of education. Their lives are in all senses much broader, more open to the world, than those of trade unionists; and, after all is said and done, their thoughts are not so much concentrated upon dividend as the thoughts of trade unionists are upon the living wage. The chief attempt at alliance between co-operation and University Extension happened some three years since. The hearts of true co-operative educators beat high; the gates of the co-operative state seemed open wide to welcome operations—the best that University Extension could offer. The gates clanged to, but not until University Extension, as such, had secured a definite stand upon the educational basis of co-operation. That stand is expressed by the arrangements for co-operators to attend the summer meeting and by the recognition and registration of properly qualified class teachers. These operations tend to act upon the individual rather than upon the movement; but it is in the nature of things that such individuals will, by reason of their superior equipment, some day direct and control the educational machinery. Then the gates will be reopened wide, to admit wise and free education in economics, history, science, and art, for the illumination of the everyday operations of a movement which is bound by the terms of its ideal to live in illumination or to pass to its own place.

Finally, it is essential to true citizenship that men should be forced beyond the veneer of a superficial elementary education, which is self-contained, and should be led to the beautiful and the true, where alone citizenship can be realized. This is the special function of University Extension; and that movement will do well to settle itself deliberately upon trade unionism and co-operation, where, in spite of opposition and dead days, it will finally see the day of fruition and be satisfied.

II. A Plan of Action

The need for the full and free action of a wise educational system upon the leading democratic movements becomes daily more imperative. This is substantiated by the remarks made by Mr. Bell in his report to the Amalgamated Society of Railway Servants upon the Taff Vale case. He complained that the members were 'not sufficiently careful in their selection of the executive committee'; that the tendency seemed to be to elect the members whom he refers to as 'irresponsible,' and 'not the most thoughtful'; but 'who have become popular through the exercise of their oratorical power.' Upon such a tendency he lays prime responsibility for the damage to prestige and the lost funds resultant upon the adverse judicial decisions in the case.

Evidence such as this, from one of the most capable of trade union leaders, must force the hands of those who would promote education. The time is now at hand. In all democratic movements, small and large, there are those among its units who have the capacity and desire to educate and be educated; men who are anxious to have their thought stimulated and quickened by placing it in the current of correct thought, in which, while receiving all, they add a quota. These are they to whom educators must look. It matters not whether they be prominent units or insignificant from the point of view of their movements, so long as they be organized for placement, locally, within the sphere of educational operations, such as those of the University Extension Society. Such organization would, without question, bring into being that corrective influence necessary to make it possible for working men to bear their legitimate burdens in municipal, national, and imperial affairs.

The initiative in the matter will best lie with the University Extension authorities on the one part, and the Co-operative movement, strengthened by an alliance with trade unionists, on the other. The semi-responsibility for such initiative accrues to University Extension, because it has recognized to the full democratic needs, and has consistently rendered its high teaching acceptable to working men. On the other hand, the Co-operative movement has rendered to education, as such, a greater measure of tribute than any other democratic movement. It has, indeed, set upon foot a system of class teaching in industrial history, economics, and citizenship. Moreover, it has entered already into a working alliance with University Extension. The division of labour between these two specified movements is not a matter of great difficulty. It would probably commend itself to the University Extension authorities to take further steps to place in the hands of working men, through the medium of co-operative societies and trade unions, a statement of their whole attitude towards the education of the working classes: as well as to promote conferences in connection with co-operative societies and trade unions (especially when those movements meet in congress), continuing, of course, the conferences which have already been held at their own summer meetings. This work would be rendered comparatively easy by the appointment of co-operators and trade unionists to act as local secretaries or co-secretaries; in such places, at least, where University Extension is already in touch with co-operative and trade union effort. The manifest duty of such secretaries would be to organize groups of working men, with a view to their definite inclusion within the University Extension centre; and perchance, under favourable circumstances, to promote and sustain a centre.

It is not suggested that existing successful co-operative classes, any more than trade union branch meetings held for educational purposes, shall necessarily place themselves within the University Extension centres; but it is suggested that it should be rendered possible for co-operative classes to have the option of existence within such centres. By this is meant that, where the subject is part and parcel of the existing or an extended curriculum of the Co-operative Union, the attendance of certified co-operative students under the auspices of the local society shall be aided by a grant, and in other ways officially recognized, even as though the attendances were made at a typical co-operative class. If this were brought about, the Co-operative movement would be in a much better position than ever before to realize its educational ideal as originally expressed by the 'Rochdale Pioneers,' and elaborated by Arnold Toynbee, to the general satisfaction of co-operators.

This organization proceeding quietly would be ultimately controlled, if constitutionally possible, by a joint committee of university extensionists, co-operators, and trade unionists; which joint committee would subordinate to itself, or exercise some control over, the various local committees founded upon the same plan. The procedure of trade unionists, in order to secure the requisite official recognition by their trade union, would necessarily be more protracted than that of co-operators, because trade unionism has no educational machinery, as such, in existence. It must, however, be remembered that the better class of trade unionists are frequently co-operators on principle.

There is no doubt that in many localities the spirit of the work is abroad waiting for the organizing touch. In the London district, the societies at Stratford and Woolwich have encouraged their members to attend the local centres, and have even stimulated them by offering valuable prizes. During the present spring term over one hundred courses are to be delivered in towns where there are co-operative societies, and certainly trade union branches.

There is, however, it must be frankly admitted, on the part of leading co-operators, an unpardonable suspicion of the university, often flavoured with contempt, and a pronounced antipathy to anything that can possibly be misconstrued into a desire on the part of any movement, educational or otherwise, pushing its own legitimate work, to exploit them. The most progressive of the younger men, however, are free from this taint, and recognize to the full that it does not matter in the least who educates so long as the education is real. At a recent conference, the most successful of their class teachers pleaded, after Emerson, that 'the co-operative wagon be hitched to the university star,' justified no doubt in his plea by his recognition of the fact that the best success of co-operative classes, in the past, has been to a great extent due to university influence.

If, then, co-operation as well as trade unionism, not excluding the lesser working-class movements, will fully trust University Extension, rendering it due recognition and reasonable assistance, in the manner heretofore suggested, they will have taken a real step towards bringing their ideals within reach of their most insignificant units, and call down upon democracy that uniting wisdom which is the necessary antecedent of high moral power.

The co-operator's vision as he contemplates the beneficent result of the linkage, by University Extension, of the great democratic movements to the abounding thought of the world (wagons to the heaven of stars) is illimitable in its vistas of promise. The deep draughts of knowledge drunk by those within the currents of correct thought will provide that power and strength which, in spite of stressful and baneful days, will divert the strong movements of the people from the narrow paths of immediate interests to the broad way of that rightly ordered social life of which only glimpses have yet been seen even by the greatest of the world's seers.

III. An Association

In his convincing book, *Education and Empire*, Mr. Haldane has written: 'Educate your people, and you have reduced to comparatively insignificant dimensions the problems of temperance, of housing, and of raising the conditions of your masses.' If this be granted, as indeed it must, the need for persistent and deliberate action on the part of teaching authorities rises to an importance that cannot well be over-estimated. Education and empire are inseparable. Education creates and sustains that empire of which it is the inner defence. It is, therefore, of imperial importance that wise and free education should operate incessantly upon the energetic movements of democracy, and once again, be it said, that University Extension is eminently fitted to bring this operation about.

The constitution of the Extension authorities by the universities, in whose keeping lies the educational heart of England, is instinct with promise for the education of democracy. At once a legitimate duty and a crowning glory lies in the absorption of the working class 'new blood' by the University Extension movement.

Stress must be laid upon the responsibility that accrues to University Extension in this matter, the sole duty of which is to educate; whereas it is not the sole duty of the democracy to seek education. The rush and stress of working-class life renders it very difficult for the units to stop to contemplate even for a moment, much less to seek, those favoured spots where education is to be found. Co-operative effort makes for dividend, frequently sadly forgetful of all else. Trade unionists concentrate upon the living wage and, at this present, upon parliamentary representation. There are many living upon a lower plane whose whole lives are prolonged struggles for bread, into which rest seldom, and thought never, enters. Surely the 'one clear call' to University Extension is that, in spite of all difficulties, it should increase its work; for, in the long run, its thought must tempt the potential thought of the democracy to leap into the open and become one with it.

Mr. Halstead, in his generous article in the last issue of this journal—an article inspired by the effect of his untiring work these many years past for democratic education—enters a plea for action, and it is becoming increasingly plain that such action will best be relegated to an association, the chief function of which will be to make ready and prepare the democratic mind for the ordinary operations of University Extension. By securing entry to the very many co-operative and trade union meetings, which are everywhere held, as well as permission to contribute articles to co-operative records and trade union journals, an association properly constituted could arrange for an illimitable amount of necessary work. In more favoured spots it could call into existence organized effort, and arrange meetings of the character specified by Mr. W. H. Brown in his useful letter in that same issue.[1] At such a time as this, however, it is not opportune to dwell upon the manifold ways which are open to legitimate and wise educational propaganda.

Keeping steadily in view the intermediary character of the proposed association, it becomes necessary to consider its possible relations to the three specified movements.

(i) *University Extension*

It is quite clear that the official sanction, if only provisional, of the University Extension movement as a whole, will be necessary to the success of the association, and it is to be reasonably expected that each of the four authorities will be represented upon an executive committee. Indeed, it is quite in accordance with the principles expressed that the association be merely a joint effort of the four authorities. Neither need there be any fear that University Extension will be cheapened—which would be disastrous—because the working officials may well be existing University Extension lecturers whose method and sympathies conform most nearly to the working-class mind.

Obviously, however, a purely self-governing association, having co-operators and trade unionists upon its executive (in effect a joint committee), would the better commend itself. Constituted in such a manner, it would inevitably be a most effective propagandist and preparatory agent for the Extension course.

[1] 'Let the University Extension committee invite the trade union committee and the leaders of co-operative education to a social meeting to meet the University Extension lecturer. At such a gathering the ideals of the latter could be put forth and discussed, and ladies and gentlemen appointed to attend trade union and co-operative meetings for missionary purposes.'

B

(ii) *The Co-operative Movement*

It is a matter for great content at the present time that the Co-operative Union officially recognizes University Extension, thanks to the indefatigable efforts of the Oxford secretary on the one part, and to a devoted band of co-operative educators on the other.   Clearly the ordinary educational operations of the Co-operative movement would be stimulated if the Extension work, which is now assisted and sometimes wholly maintained by co-operators—such work as that reported at Cleator Moor in the April issue of this journal—were officially recognized, encouraged, and recorded.   Mr. Halstead expresses the difficulty accruing to the isolated student; but surely the society to which the student belongs could apply for his official recognition, and his attendance at the University Extension centre could be registered, without great difficulty, in accordance with the regulations of the Co-operative Union.   In reference to the financial difficulty, it is to be assumed that the Co-operative Union is anxious for an extension of its class teaching and would willingly be responsible for the additional financial burden involved.

The general assistance of co-operative classes, especially those taught by co-operators recognized as teachers by the Oxford Delegacy, arises amongst other matters, wherein a joint association could materially assist the educational work of co-operation, which has been part and parcel of the movement since its foundation.

(iii) *Trade Unionism*

As previously pointed out, trade unionism has no educational machinery, as such, in existence, although useful work is done in connection with many branches.   If it be admitted that the general run of trade unionists are indifferent to extra educational effort, yet it must also be admitted that the leaders—who know only too well that their real power entirely depends upon the measure of correct thought behind them—will rejoice if any educational effort which promises persistence is brought in contact with trade unionism. It is, indeed, a worthy object for any educational body to seek to exert educational influence upon such powerful organizations as many of the unions are. The ultimate constitutional relationship will, of necessity, depend upon the degree of constructive influence which can be brought to bear upon trade unionism in the future.

In order fully to test the proposals herein made, it will probably be well for a pioneer association to be initiated, which will so work as to endeavour to render a permanent association inevitable. The first work of such a pioneer association, after issuing a manifesto, would be exhaustively to survey the whole field as it exists, and report thereon. Starting in the immediate future, it could secure approval at a joint conference of co-operators, trade unionists, and university extensionists; to be held in the late summer or autumn under the auspices of one, or all, of the University Extension authorities.

This series of articles may well conclude with a strong expression of real hope that a forward movement will result, if not on the actual lines indicated, yet on some modification of them; for such a movement will inevitably benefit University Extension and democracy alike, and express itself in increasing contributions to the correct thought of our time.

2. WORKING MEN AND CONTINUATION SCHOOLS

(This was written in 1907, and was a contribution to a volume entitled *Continuation Schools in England and Elsewhere,* edited by Michael Sadler and published by the Manchester University Press. A full survey is given of the progress of continuative education at that time, as carried out by the Co-operative movement. Suggestions are made as to how continuative education can be made more attractive to the children leaving the day school. Reference is made to the work of the Workers' Educational Association at that period.)

THERE is at present a strong current of interest in education among the skilled workers in England. It is felt that more must be done not only to improve the conditions of work in the ordinary elementary schools, but to provide some form of further education for boys and girls who have completed the elementary school course. So far as I can judge, however, the idea of enforcing attendance at evening continuation classes without also limiting the hours of employment of all young people up to seventeen years of age is regarded with less favour than was the case two or three years ago. Discussion of the question has disclosed many practical difficulties.

For the purpose of an inquiry into the attitude of working men towards evening continuation schools, the term 'working men' may be held to include not only artisans and those who work for an hourly wage, but desk clerks and those who work for a salary; not only those whose skill alone is their necessary qualification, but those who, when changing employment, need written references.

If the term 'working men' be considered in its narrow and legal aspect, then those embraced by it can be isolated only through the trade unions of the country, which themselves include but a part of those eligible to join them.

The Friendly Society movement cannot be considered 'working class' unless the whole body of clerks be included in the term. The Co-operative movement has in it representatives of all classes.

To turn to another aspect of the question, artisans may be divided into three classes: those whose intention it is to become foremen, those who are filled with the spirit of combination — trade unionists before all else — and those who are satisfied simply to do their day's work. The first class will secure technical education at all costs; it is represented in our polytechnics by many keen students who study the theory of their trades. The best of the representatives of the second class are frequently to be found amongst those who study economics, industrial history, and citizenship. An artisan seldom finds his interests in both of these classes; if so, it is not for long. In the third class the great body of artisans may be placed. It supplies the rank and file of the trade unions. It is the class that, even above the others, needs the influences of a wise and careful propaganda. It has seldom expressed itself educationally. It is far in the rear of its leaders. From it the general impression that artisans are careless of their higher educational interest has been gained. Men of this class are unwilling to submit themselves to any definite educational influences, but when they are organized they will fall into line with that modern working-class movement which is definitely and distinctly educational. This movement, clearly expressed, as it is, by the leaders, is to be counted upon as a factor in the future. Workpeople as a whole are seeing more and more clearly that education is the great thing and the real thing, making all things possible for the man who has it.

The desk clerk, who is often a member of an artisan's family, demands consideration. His work is simply to write plainly; to add correctly; to use a ready reckoner; and to exercise the ordinary virtues of punctuality and amenability to discipline. More thoughtful members of this class attend continuation schools for the purpose of gaining proficiency in shorthand, typewriting, and book-keeping. In this way they increase their value during the early years of their employment, and are better equipped when opportunities for promotion occur. The ordinary clerk is not studious. He does not attend continuation schools and does not desire to do so. It may be argued that he must be quite aware of the fact that wage-earning power increases with knowledge, but this fact is often obscured by the conditions of work in a large office, and by the lack of necessary inspiration in a small one. Moreover, the obtrusively studious type of clerk seldom gets promotion, certainly not more rapidly than the man who does not study. It is the well-balanced clerk who succeeds; the clerk who is educated in a real way, so that the facts of his knowledge and his certificates do not obtrude themselves; his knowledge showing itself—and all true knowledge should—in character and general efficiency. The average clerk does not understand this. He sees the man who is obviously studious still working at the desk, and fails to see that the man who succeeds has been, of necessity, studious also, though in a different way. In a large office in London, directly connected with the Co-operative movement, it was found that only a very small proportion of the clerks had ever attended evening continuation schools, and these, almost without exception, for the purpose of studying shorthand and book-keeping. The organization, in this case, true to its profession, directly encourages employees, offering to pay their fees for classes in general and technical subjects at University Extension courses, colleges, and polytechnics. The applications made are few. In 1903–4 only twenty-eight applications were received from over a thousand employees, and even when there was a direct technical connection between the classes and the daily work the same state of affairs prevailed. Those who had attended evening continuation schools were asked what they thought necessary to increase the efficiency of such schools. The unanimous answer was 'more social opportunities,' although some felt that the efficiency of evening school work depended to a very great extent upon smaller classes and more individual instruction. It must be remembered that book-keeping, shorthand, and typewriting classes are always well filled and frequently overcrowded.

This brief consideration of the conditions of artisans and desk clerks leads directly to the conclusion that there is great

need for a propaganda which would insist upon its being the
duty of every artisan to educate himself to the utmost of his
capacity in order to be of greater service to the community.
It should appeal to him to continue his education, to increase
his efficiency, to add to his possibilities, not only for himself,
but for the sake of the community to which he belongs.   Much
educational propaganda in the past has failed because its expressions have been unintelligible to working men.   Moreover, there is great danger of the materialistic appeal being
given undue prominence.   Artisans and clerks have been
appealed to for many years to educate themselves with the
object of improving their positions.   Where the appeal has
been answered it has certainly not been followed by the same
success that a larger appeal might have induced: an appeal
directed not to motives which might easily become selfish,
but to such motives as are included in the man whose measure
and stature are perfect.

The efforts of working men in connection with evening
continuation schools must be treated entirely as the work of
co-operators.   The Trade Union movement, as such, has
had until late years no direct connection with educational
movements.[1]   The reason for this is not far to seek.   The
work of the trade unions has been peculiarly definite.   They
have concerned themselves with such matters as the improvement of the status of their members, the maintenance of the
standard rate of wages, and the financial operations of sick
and other benefits.   The very definiteness of those objects
has prevented the conception of a larger ideal.   Owing,
however, to the influence of trades councils, and the advanced position of many of their leaders, they are now asso-
ciating themselves with educational movements.   They are
to be counted upon as factors in any work which tends to
increase the efficiency of popular education; their representatives are to be seen at educational conferences; their

---

[1] Some branches of the Northern Counties Weavers' Association, however,
have for many years encouraged the attendance of their younger members at
technical classes by payment of fees and by rewards. This action has been
successful in stimulating the educational interest of the younger members
concerned.

support has been generously given to the Workers' Educational Association and to such institutions as the Ruskin College at Oxford; moreover their papers and magazines are always open to educational influences. When occasion demands the leaders never fail to express the importance of education to working men. The educationist who would estimate the forces of the future would be wrong if he omitted the trade unions, although in his estimate of the past he is unable to grant them, in this immediate connection, high place.

Working men's clubs have, in many instances, maintained work of an educational character, although more frequently their work has been in connection with local or national politics. Friendly societies of all types have been usually content with the excellence of their financial operations. On the other hand, the Social Democratic Federation, the Fabian Society, and Clarion Clubs have never failed to propagate their ideals by means of definite teaching. Fabian book-boxes have always been in great demand; Socialist Sunday schools for adults have done useful work, and of late years the Adult School movement has made much progress, even inducing the suggestion that continuation school education might in some way be attached to Sunday schools.

In a recent speech Mr. D. J. Shackleton, M.P., stated that he received his early education at classes in connection with a co-operative society. This is a significant and typical fact. The Co-operative movement has been in contact with popular education at many points. It has been frequently a pioneer. Its work in connection with free libraries ceased only when the municipalities commenced to take action. A large number of co-operative societies have kept true to the old ideal, 'educate your members,' clearly expressed by the Rochdale Pioneers in 1844. Their work in connection with evening continuation schools has sometimes been sufficient for the locality, and has often paved the way for municipal action. The admission must be made, however, that most of the educational work of the Co-operative movement during later years has been propagated, not by working-men co-operators, but by men of the educated class who have become co-operators.

The educational report of the Co-operative Union would mislead an inquirer who was not alive to the fact that only a portion of the educational work of the movement is recorded therein.   It is customary to base criticisms on this report. The report, however, deals only with such work as lies immediately within the sphere of influence of the Central Education Committee of the Union.   During the year 1905 the sum of £83,266 was voted for educational work by co-operative societies, independently of the Central Committee.   A great part of this sum, no doubt, was spent upon advertisements and social functions, but many societies paid continuation school fees for their members and their members' children. Some societies expend a large amount every year in this way.

Turning directly to the subject of the inquiry, it is interesting at the outset to take a few typical examples of societies which pay fees.   During the session 1902–3 Norwich Society paid the fees of seventy-five students; but in the session 1903–4 no fees were paid unless the students had been approved by examination.   Only ten students were so approved.   The Ipswich Co-operative Society agreed to pay fees at the Technical Institute during 1903–4.   The fees of twelve men studying technical subjects and the fees of twenty women studying domestic subjects were paid.   The Oldham Industrial Society (Lancashire) pays half of the fees charged to members and their children, but the amount paid for each individual is not allowed to exceed five shillings.   The York Co-operative Society paid, in 1903–4, for over six hundred students, who, for the most part, attended science classes. It may be remarked that very few co-operative societies of standing exclude themselves from the educational work of the town or district in which they are situated.   It is especially satisfactory to record that their approval of evening school work is supplemented so often by financial assistance.   This assistance has been generous and genuine, and it may safely be inferred that if the municipality had not taken steps to establish classes, the co-operative society would often have done so.   The cases in which co-operative societies have acted as evening continuation school authorities for the town

* B

are not numerous. The minutes of the Grays Co-operative Society (Essex) are instructive. In 1884—it may be noted that the London School Board did no evening school work between the years 1875 and 1882—free elementary classes were held in the Co-operative Assembly Rooms at Grays on two evenings per week. These were continued up to 1887, but no Government grant was claimed. In 1885–6 a teacher was engaged to teach technical subjects. In 1887 classes were commenced by the society in connection with South Kensington. The subjects taught were geometry, building construction, drawing, mathematics, magnetism and electricity, botany, and geology. The teachers were duly qualified men. The outcome was that a Technical Instruction Board was formed in the town, which purchased the whole teaching stock of the co-operative society. The Plymouth society, another interesting example, gained Government grants up to the year 1897–8, when it voluntarily relinquished them, while continuing the education if its members in the study of industrial history and economics. Its classes have been for many years the most successful held under the auspices of the Education Committee of the Co-operative Union. The schools of the local authority at Plymouth are also well attended and successful.

Some co-operative societies which held continuation schools up to the passing of the 1902 Act have now handed them over to the local authority. Of these the Preston schools demand special notice, not only because of the large attendance, but because of the excellent way in which the schools were arranged to prepare students for the instruction given at the Harris Institute in the town. The children were caught by the co-operative society before they had time to forget what they had learnt at the day school, and numbers were passed on to the higher institution, frequently assisted by the payment of their fees. The status of the committee as an educational body was admitted by the inclusion of its representative on the Preston education authority. The ideal of the society was expressed in its official *Record* for April 1903:

For the last six years half the householders (co-operators) of Preston have agreed to open evening schools each winter for the benefit, not merely of those belonging to the society, but for *all* the young people in the town who chose to attend them, or adults whose education had been neglected.   Time, money, and thought have been freely expended, but we have never grudged the outlay of any of these valuable commodities; for we have fondly dreamt that we were building up a fair structure on a good and lasting foundation.   We believed that the present and future generations of young people, through our efforts on their behalf, would, when they grew to man and womanhood, raise the standard of knowledge, honour, and purity in our town.

The grant from the Board of Education in 1902–3 amounted to £1,000; in 1903–4 to £1,936.   The secretary reported that the average attendance for 1902–3 was 2,129, while the largest attendance on one evening was 2,492.   In 1903–4 the average had increased to 2,500.   This, says the secretary, was probably not excelled by the record of any other classes in the kingdom.   It may be noted that the average attendance at thirty-three Liverpool schools was, in 1903–4, 4,780.   The estimated population of Liverpool in 1903 was 716,810, of Preston 114,404.   The high average at Preston was, no doubt, to a great extent induced by a carefully graduated system of rewards, ranging from 'thirty-one attendances, trip for a shilling' to 'forty-two attendances (highest possible), all fees returned, prize, and trip free'; but this is a consideration that may be passed over in view of the fact that 712 students sat for the examination of the Lancashire and Cheshire Union in 1904, and of these 596 passed, 326 of them in arithmetic. Such excellent results fully justified the remarks of Sir William Tomlinson, who, taking 'London' as his text at the close of the 1902–3 session, said:

It was evident that the evening continuation schools in Preston were supplying a great want in our English system of education.   Sir John Gorst had devoted much time to the review of the work accomplished in the evening schools in connection with the London board schools, and the result of his research had not been altogether satisfactory.   Possibly this was due to the quality of the teaching in the London board schools; possibly it was not quite in touch with the future life of the scholars.   Frequently there was a total break when they left the day schools, and the result was that what had been learned was quickly forgotten.   A great difficulty was found in inducing these young people to attend the evening schools, or, when they did so, to pay proper attention.   One reason for this probably was that they had had a hard day's work previously, and were half asleep, and unable to apply themselves to serious study.   There was a want, too, of organization, which evidently was not the case in Preston, and the co-operative society was to be congratulated on the serious manner in which its members and the Educational Committee had taken up the cause of education, and supplied the link in the chain which the half-time system so often broke. It was pleasing to find that the society had been able to bring so many young people to see the advantage of a better education, and the harmony which existed between these classes and those of the Harris Institute was another excellent feature.

The record attendance for any one evening was made in the 1903–4 session, when 3,246 students attended sixty-nine classes, an average of forty-seven students per class. The future of continuation school work in Preston has been placed beyond all doubt by the action of co-operators. The secretary's manifesto, published upon the opening of the seventh session, ran as follows:

It is our pleasure to be able to record a very large increase in the number of students in attendance.

As the new education authority in Preston do not feel themselves in a position to take over the classes at present, they have expressed a desire that we should continue them for the present session. What the future has in store for our classes we cannot say. Should the new authority take them under their own control we will endeavour to assist them in every possible way.[1]

The future of evening classes will be very much what the students make it. It will be the duty of the new authority to satisfy the educational requirements of our town; therefore we desire to impress upon all students who have enrolled themselves at our schools this session the importance of attending as regularly as possible, in order to show that there is a demand for such classes in Preston.

It is a pleasing feature to notice the large number of youths and maidens who have lately left the day schools attending our evening schools. This is as it should be; we feel sure that when they arrive at years of discretion they will be better men and women for their early studies.

At St. Helens the co-operative society, which has carried on its classes for several years, decided to continue them under the existing Act. In 1903–4, 300 students of upwards of sixteen years of age attended the classes. The teachers are

---

[1] The schools were handed over to the local authority at the commencement of the 1905–6 session. Writing on 22nd May 1906 the Director of Education for Preston gave the average attendance for the session as 1,250 at sixty-six classes held in sixteen schools. This showed a serious falling off from the average attendance of 2,500 in 1903–4, to be accounted for, no doubt, partly by the discontinuance of the system of rewards described above, as also by the necessary leakage occasioned by the transfer to a new authority and the withdrawal of the idea of the co-operative store behind the schools.

those chiefly employed in day schools, and the annual cost to the society is from £80 to £100. The secretary reports 'that the classes have been very successful, and the students, who are mostly the sons and daughters of working men, have manifested great interest in the work, and the higher Government grant has always been earned.'

A successful evening school, with an average attendance of 355 during 1903–4, is conducted by the Coventry Co-operative Society. The Government reports are consistently congratulatory in tone. Professor Hughes stated that 'the schools constitute a distinct benefit to the whole city.'[1] Among the subjects taught are 'hand and eye training,' 'knowledge of common things,' citizenship, and literature. It is satisfactory to note the praise awarded to these classes by His Majesty's inspector. The objects of the society in carrying on these evening schools are clearly expressed:

(a) To continue and supplement the elementary teaching of the day schools, and

(b) To form a connecting link between the day schools and the more advanced science, art, language, and technology classes of the municipal school of art and technical school.

Amongst other societies which have carried on evening school work earning Government grants are Mirfield (Yorkshire), Langley Mill, Leigh (Lancashire), Oldham Industrial (Lancashire), Rugby, and Rochdale Pioneers (Lancashire). The Oldham and Rochdale societies discontinued their work some time ago, expressing the opinion that such work belonged to the municipality. It is not probable that any co-operative society will, in the future, set up continuation schools. At the Stratford Congress, May 1904, Mr. W. R. Rae, chairman of the Education Committee of the Co-operative Union, said:

As to evening schools and science and art classes, I advise societies not to rush into the supply of either. The local authority for education may undertake to do it, and levy a rate for maintenance. Our duty is plain, viz. to see that they do theirs, and perhaps also to see that we are adequately represented on the body and our views made known.

In the discussion which followed this view was endorsed,

[1] Report on the Educational Resources of the City. Coventry, 1904.

and the resolution passed at the conclusion contained these words:

> This Congress earnestly recommends societies to concentrate their efforts on the formation of co-operative character and opinion, rather than to carry on work or any portion of work which is more correctly the work of the local or municipal authority.

Although but few societies will be directly represented on local education authorities, and these probably confined to Lancashire, there is a strong tendency on the part of co-operators, as such, to strive at local elections for representation. This tendency will probably merge itself into the general movement for labour representation, which is making it possible for an increasing number of workmen to sit upon bodies that control education, from Parliament downwards. The workmen's bench in the London County Council is well represented upon the working sub-committees on education. Very many working men are doing similar work in different parts of England. Labour men who condemned the provisions of the London Bill before it was passed are now endeavouring to secure that it shall be administered in the light of a progressive theory. They stand for smaller classes and for free evening schools. Labour will not be parsimonious in educational policy. Imperial taxation must pay for it (*vide* resolution, Trade Union Congress, September 1907). The defence it would have for the nation is 'brains' in preference to 'armaments,' but it must again be remembered that the policy is expressed by the leaders, and not by the rank and file.

Now that apprenticeship is practically a dead letter, there is a strong feeling that something should take its place, and the something must surely be a system of education persisted in after the boy has begun to work at his craft. Very quickly after he begins work a boy forgets what he learned at school, and often at eighteen or nineteen turns to the evening schoolmaster and to the technical instructor destitute of the elements of arithmetic. No greater waste in an educational system can be imagined than that which in ours takes place between the ages of fourteen and eighteen, or, it may be said, after fourteen; because many lads never even ask the technical schools to teach them elementary arithmetic.   Out of fourteen lads who presented themselves at the book-keeping class of a London evening school in September 1904 two were unable to decide the total cost of three articles at eleven shillings each.   The ignorance of students who desire to study shorthand and typewriting, if not so obvious, is not less real. In one of the excellent Preston schools the inspector suggests that 'it would be a great advantage if instruction in shorthand could be preceded by a thorough grounding in English.'

It is not the healthy, strong, energetic boy who readily attends evening school; it is often the boy of unenterprising temperament.   The former boy attends, if anything, the church guild or the lads' brigade.   He finds complete satisfaction in the social intercourse provided by the members of his cricket or football club.   He follows healthy, clean courses, but is out of line with systematic intellectual training at the most critical period of his life.

It has been an interesting experience to work in a large office during the day, and to teach in a continuation school at night.   The result has been to assure one over and over again that the lad who has really the greatest need of school seldom attends.   The great majority of the boys who leave the elementary day schools never come on to the evening school at all, or only do so when they have forgotten much that they learnt, and find that their future advancement is blocked unless they recover lost ground.   Many of the brightest boys are amongst those who thus stay away.   One must confess that some of those who meritoriously come on to the evening school directly after leaving the day school are a rather tame and uninteresting type, though it seems a shame to say so. Sometimes a sharp junior, whose employer has suggested shorthand to him, is there; sometimes a man of mature years, who works patiently and frequently successfully, and is a real joy to the teacher.   It sometimes happens that a social group, which usually exists outside the school, drifts in, and an unpopular class, such as 'commercial history,' may suddenly find itself augmented by a round dozen.   The great disadvantage is that if one member leaves the whole group follows.

It has frequently been suggested that the type of education given in elementary schools to working lads, with its strict discipline, and on occasion its personal coercion, induces a distaste for school surroundings that nothing but compulsion can be expected to overcome; and it must not be forgotten that to a lad it is a great thing to gain even that moderate freedom to move about and talk which a workshop or an office affords. Such a state of affairs is in itself a new life.

But, after all, cannot more boys and girls be led to attend evening schools irrespective of compulsion? We think they can, and a few suggestions as to the means may fitly close this inquiry. But first let us say that we do not blind our eyes to the disabilities placed in the way of many young people by the conditions of their employment. Only 'compulsion,' exercised through the employers, can remove such disabilities, and it is for this reason, chiefly, that we should support a measure of statutory obligation to remove them.

No scholars should be allowed to leave the day school without distinct attempts being made to ensure that they have ideas suitable to their age upon the importance of education.

First, they should possess the sheet-anchor of a clear knowledge as to the precise meaning and importance of the three R's. The door of the treasure house of the world should be opened before them, and the key to it, they should understand, is education. It should be impressed upon them that they have hardly begun to 'know'; that copy-book maxims and statements such as 'knowledge is power' are profound truths. The distinct benefits of evening school education should be explained to them, together with the reasons why it has been set on foot, what it has done, and all in the light of the great principle that it is a boy's duty to use his brains for the sake of his country.

Secondly, the municipal spirit should be fostered; it is always ready to spring into growth. The evening school should be, as far as possible, the instrument of a social institution for which the boy or girl has already a liking or respect. Evening schools in connection with co-operative societies have been successful, in part because there was the idea of the store behind them. In like manner the idea of the municipality must be behind the school. The experiment made by the late London School Board of teaching local history to scholars was a step in this direction.

Thirdly, the theory of discipline and the dignity of voluntarily submitting to it as *organization* should be explained.

With these principles thoroughly instilled, there is no reason why the average boy should not normally pass to the evening school, especially if guilds, lads' brigades, and clubs can be induced to work together with the eeucation authority. Above all things boys and girls must never be urged to study merely for their own advancement. Those who have a personal ambition can be trusted to look well after their opportunities.

The curriculum of the evening schools should conform as nearly as possible to a line drawn somewhat higher than the line of daily work. For example, a carpenter's boy should not be taught merely to plane and chisel, but he should be educated in the true spirit of the craft. He should be steeped in its tradition, and shown old and beautiful work, being taught at the same time how to appraise it. The relation of his craft to other crafts and to the world of industry should be clearly demonstrated. Again, the commercial evening school, besides training the young clerk to be a good shorthand writer and a good book-keeper, should try to kindle his interest in economic questions and his sense of citizenship. Working lads must be educated as whole boys, not merely as sections. It is desirable that education authorities should arrange to have placed at least once a session before evening scholars a clear statement as to the history, meaning, and purpose of evening school education. This would tend to steady the attendance, because it would give definiteness of aim to pupils who previously lacked it. Evening schools should always have at least one room where workmen and boys can, without hindrance, work independently of the teacher—do homework, in fact. Many homes in which respectable artisans live—not overcrowded—are inconvenient for the purpose. In two-room tenements one would imagine work to be impossible. A bright room—and the expectation that the responsible teacher would look in to solve the knotty problems—would help working men in their studies to an extent which they only could appreciate.

To carry out the reforms which these suggestions indicate would involve some expenditure of public money. It would become increasingly necessary that a staff of evening school teachers should be raised. The quality of the teaching in day and evening schools must suffer when the work is carried on by the same people. A number of business men teach in evening schools and, although they gather freshness and strength from the change of employment, the teaching and the teacher suffer if both teaching and business are persisted in. It is a present-day problem how to secure sufficient day school teachers. The greater problem of evening school teachers must inevitably be faced. Evening school teachers might suitably teach their *special* subjects in day schools for a portion of the day.

Working-class opinion is developing on the subject of further education, and the efforts of the Workers' Educational Association have been not without influence in giving definition to somewhat vague educational ideals. The chief object of the association is to arouse among the workers greater interest in higher education, and to direct their attention to the facilities already provided. Its branches are at work ascertaining the needs and wishes of the workers, and in many places (notably in Rochdale, Reading, Birmingham, and High Wycombe) have co-operated with the local authorities and with university organizations in securing the better provision of educational opportunities congenial to the industrial classes. At the Preston Co-operative Congress in 1907 a speaker thus described the aims and work of the association:

Necessary as it is for England to develop, in every way that may be possible, the technical training of the worker for his work: necessary as it is that such training should be closely associated with the workshop and with the practical conditions of the trades; we believe that side by side with this technical training there should go, for the workers not less than for the leisured, an education in the humanities, an education which touches the imagination, the heart, and the conscience. The Workers' Educational Association stands for this broad and humanizing ideal, and in striving for that ideal it is being faithfully and unselfishly served. It has, moreover, a further claim on our regard. It does not emphasize educational differences: it seeks rather to appease and assuage them. It does not set itself up as a rival and as a competitor with other kinds of educational effort. On the contrary, it draws attention in each district to the various forms of educational opportunity which already exist. It brings together, to a united work, the isolated men and women who are ready to respond to the claims of education for social duty, and who wish to learn in order that they may be more effective in the work of social reform.

3. UNIVERSITY TUTORIAL CLASSES

(In July 1912 the universities of the British Empire met in congress in London. This address was delivered before the assembly, and later published in the proceedings of the congress, by the University of London Press. A survey is given of the work of the Workers' Educational Association in England, and mention is made of the need for the founding of a central library to supply books to students. The empire universities were invited to form joint committees to promote higher education for working men.)

I DESIRE first to pay my tribute to the memory of Dr. R. D. Roberts, who devoted the finest energies, during a distinguished career, to the cause of the education of the people.

It is generally admitted in these days that universities should draw their strength from all worthy activities in the national life, and it is recognized that the activities of working men and women stand amongst the most important of them. It has, indeed, the most numerous adherents. The University Tutorial Class movement is one of the contributions towards full and complete co-operation between working men and women as such, and scholars as such.

The University Tutorial Class consists of thirty adult men and women, pledged to study for three years, and not to miss a single attendance other than from unavoidable causes, and to write twelve essays in connection with each of the three sessions of twenty-four lessons each; together with one tutor, who must be a fine scholar, and whose main business in life is the development of the subject with which he deals.

Its essential characteristic is freedom. The students control the class, the justification for which is that they have devised for themselves regulations which are of greater severity than any which a university would have dreamed of asking them to frame. It is *the* class of the students—each student is a teacher, and each teacher is a student; the humblest is not afraid to teach, and the most advanced is willing to learn. There is a complete absence of distinctions; diplomas and degrees are not asked for, consequently there is no competition, but in actual fact an all-pervading comradeship.

With regard to attendance, the students have kept their

pledges wonderfully. The percentage of attendance is often over ninety per cent. It is sometimes just on a hundred per cent, which figure it has only fallen short of because of illness and overtime. The average attendance works out at seventy-five per cent, and this during a period in which there have been two general elections and violent Labour unrest. Nearly seven hundred students have completed three years' courses. The average stands at just over fifteen such students in each class which has completed its three years' courses. In towns where labour is steady, such as dockyard towns, the average rises to twenty students who have completed a three years' course. The students are almost entirely manual workers, and cover all manual trades; the textile and engineering industries make a big contribution, whilst representatives of less important occupations, such as pedlar, are numerous. The ages of the students range in the main between twenty-five and thirty, and there are several over sixty years of age. One man over seventy years of age has attracted the special commendation of Professor Vinogradoff. The Tutorial Class brought such a man for the first time into contact with scholars dealing with his subject.

As to the standard, it is true that most of the students have not attended evening schools, and have left the day schools at an early age—anything from ten to fourteen. Although used to speaking in public, they are not so used to expression by means of the written word. Spelling is often defective, but it is not always very good amongst undergraduates. Those who have examined the essays written in the classes say that the improvement in technical detail seems to be miraculous. The essays written in eight classes were examined at the close of the first year at Oxford, and twenty-five per cent of them were declared to be of a standard similar to those essays written by students who gain first-class honours in the final schools of modern history, and some essays written in these classes are circulated amongst undergraduates working for the final honours school, in order that they may read and inwardly digest them. The workman-scholar has, through these classes, revealed himself, and vindicated the claims of his order, the noblest through the ages.   The Board of Education, as stated by readers of the paper, has, through Professor L. T. Hobhouse and Mr. J. W. Headlam, reported most favourably on the classes in the light of the claim that they are equivalent to an honours course in the same subject in a university.

Thirty-nine classes have now completed three years' work. A number of them have asked for, and been granted, fourth year's courses in a special division of their subject.   One class has completed its fifth year's work, and its membership is largely intact.   Universities are devising special facilities for advanced students.   The University of Manchester has appointed an adviser of studies; the University of London is sending some of its students to the London School of Economics, and providing a seminar and special tutors for others.   The University of Oxford has always before it the question of drafting students to the university itself, and has devised a two months' summer school.   That summer school is, indeed, a most joyous occasion, and it is one of the most inspiring sights I have ever seen to see learned professors of world-wide fame studying their subject from a new point of view with the help of working people.   I need hardly say that, if any member of this congress visits Oxford, he can be assured of a welcome at the Oxford summer schools.

The classes produce teachers as well as lecturers in innumerable British working-class institutions.   It has been recorded of educational movements in the past that men would go five or six miles to a lesson.   We are able to report, in addition to this, that men will now go twelve miles to help their fellow workpeople with their class work.   The class at Longton, in the Potteries, which has finished its fifth year's course, has, by the aid of its students, maintained educational facilities in ten mining villages of north Staffordshire throughout the winter, and not a penny has been paid to the tutors, who, though poor, have cheerfully borne their own expenses. A healthy Tutorial Class develops classes round about it.

The problems gather round the supply of tutors, finance,

and the supply of books—which last is largely financial. In regard to the supply of tutors, the Board of Education has pointed out that one or two weak or tactless teachers might give a serious set-back to the movement. It is true that we claim that, just as the tutor educates the student, so the students educate the tutors, and it is interesting to note that we have tried experiments in the education of tutors, sometimes successful, sometimes unsuccessful, but an actual university tutor gains in power almost at once after he has had a little experience in teaching a Tutorial Class. Such tutors not only discover facts, but a new spirit. They take back treasures to their own university. It is true to say that the supply of tutors has been more efficient and complete than was anticipated at the outset of the movement. With one or two notable exceptions, all the tutors have succeeded—some wonderfully so— and, as a direct result of the demand for tutors, men are being prepared for the work during their undergraduate or immediately post-graduate course. Tutors must be paid a wage that will enable them to continue the work with content, and a larger wage than has often been paid to junior lecturers in universities. The working people who helped to devise the scheme said that a man should earn £400 per annum if he took five classes, and Oxford, at least, pays this amount.

The finance of the classes is arranged upon a triple basis— University, Board of Education, and Local Education Authority. There have been few private donations. Large sums are needed and, apart from the fact that the universities, recognizing the value of the work, will be glad to devote more money to it, yet new universities in England are starved (I could not help thinking of the pitiable amount which Principal Peterson spoke of, of £150,000 as the Treasury grant to them), and in some way, through the State or through the local authorities, larger finance must come to the movement; but, although finance in England follows very slowly, yet finance must, in the long run, shape itself according to the spirit of a people.

The supply of books presents a special problem, and arrangements have now been completed by which a central library has been established, the aim of which will be to circulate just at the points where they are needed expensive books of reference. The library awaits its endowment, but, at the same time, it is getting on with its useful work.

The fear of politics is not wholly dissipated, but it is true that the students have everywhere pursued their studies in the spirit of education, and have left the advocacy of their creed or party for other times and other places.

Lord Rosebery said: 'We require honourable, incorruptible, strenuous men.' We claim for the Tutorial Class movement that it creates and reveals such men, and, at the same time, gives to ordinary men what is more important—the power to select the right men. Lord Curzon bore testimony to the effect it had upon tutors of the University of Oxford—in his lordship's eyes, the very centre of all things pertaining to universities. The principal of the University of London gave as his opinion to the British Association that the classes would affect the teaching of English in universities, and Professor Pollard, speaking to the Historical Association, said that working people were forcing historians to study the lives of ordinary people. Working men, he said, were not interested so directly in the literature and art of Greece as in how the common people lived. We feel, after five years of the work, that it has strengthened the teaching of social science and history, and, to a smaller degree, of literature, in the universities of England.

It may be that some of you are delegates from universities which exist in favoured places, where it is possible for every boy and girl of brains and character to get university education. Even so, in some way or other, men and women fitted for industrial avocations, and who mature late intellectually, will need your help, and you will need theirs. The right activity of industrial labour will give them mental and spiritual gifts which you will profit by drawing to yourselves. In England we talk of a highway of education, but, when that highway is complete, we shall still need the bypaths of the Tutorial Classes.

It only remains for me to say that the universities of England and Wales have, almost without exception, recognized the value of these classes, and the majority of them have joint committees, consisting of an equal number of work-people and of representatives of the university, and I hope it may be possible, in some universities of the empire at least, that the whole question may be considered by such joint committees similarly constructed. If such joint com-mittees declared that there was nothing to be done, still, at all events, the association of workpeople and the univer-sities will have had good effect, and the desire for the welfare of the universities should be deeply embedded in the hearts of the whole population, even of those who are not fitted for university education. The universities have likewise con-structed for their common purpose a joint committee, which is, I believe, the only body in Great Britain which is repre-sentative of all the universities and university colleges of England and Wales. I think I may safely speak for that body and say that any university which desires to have copies of the papers which are circulated to its members will be welcome to them, and the Central Joint Committee will place itself at the disposal of any university which desires information.

It is a matter of satisfaction to me to-day to rejoice in the fact that overseas universities of the empire, through their association with the federation of the Workers' Educational Association, have directly aided this work. We refer to the universities of Melbourne, Sydney, and Adelaide and to McGill University. They have helped, not so much by the intrinsic value of their subscriptions—useful as those are—as by the spirit which has prompted them to cover over and aid this movement.

Even if, as Lord Curzon desires, the universities of the empire are to look to Oxford and Cambridge as 'the hills whence cometh their help,' some of us suspect that they are not the only hills, but that there are others of exceeding beauty and power, and not the least among them are many of the universities of the empire represented at this congress.

4. EDUCATION AND WORSHIP

(During the 1914–18 war, the Society for Promoting Christian Knowledge published a series of pamphlets called Wartime Tracts for the Workers. This is No. 18 of the series, and was written in 1916. In the first instance, an appeal is made on behalf of workers, that they may be given the work for which they are best fitted, and receive a just wage. Man is brought to the full worship of God as he becomes more wholly educated. Finally, a call is made to the workers to dedicate themselves and their work to the things of the spirit.)

LET there be no mistake about it. Working men and women are keen to make the best of themselves. They long for purity as for health. Self-sacrifice is the condition of their lives. Their response to an educational message rightly delivered to them is eager and persistent. The ideal of their lives is the service of their fellow men. With a little encouragement they lift up their heads and worship God, in whom as a rule they profoundly believe.

It is true that they are for the most part outside the Church. They seek to realize their religious aspirations by means of the social and industrial organizations which they have created. Many of them, however, drift hither and thither, victims of those false and vicious forces which have been let loose as a direct result of humanity organizing itself apart from God.

To Every Man his Work

The first step to be taken by those who would see education and worship paramount in the lives of the workers is towards securing for them the work for which they are fitted and an efficiency wage for their labour.

As it is, far too few get the work for which God fitted them. The kind of life our civilization has built up demands too many fetchers and carriers. Boys who have real gifts drift into blind-alley occupations and lose their morale, whilst in spite of the so-called 'educational ladder' there is little serious attempt on the part of our educational system to discover the gifts of boys and girls and to develop them. This is a problem which has been brought into relief by the Great War, and therefore stands a better chance of being worked at than it did.

Better-off parents have fallen into the error of selecting apparently desirable occupations for their children, whether they are fitted for them or not. They are tempted to do so because the world looks down on much necessary work and up to much that is artificial and unnecessary. Moreover, it is a happier thing for a man to be a skilful navvy than a clumsy doctor, and much better for those who come into contact with him.

We want to create a social order in which there will be no need to ask such questions as these: 'How can a child born and bred in that vile slum ever lead a decent life, much less find Christ and serve Him?' 'How can that man, over-worked, overstrained, underpaid, ever find time to think about God, much less to worship Him?' In the mystery of things many such children of the slums and weary men do find their way to the worship of God. They are indeed, after all, perhaps not so sadly hindered as those who farm the slums or deny the labourer his hire.

TRUE EDUCATION

Education has for its end and aim the right ordering of human life. It brings body and mind into unity with the spirit and so makes fullness of worship possible.

By far the larger part of a man's education comes through his daily work. If he has the opportunity to develop his God-given powers on the daily round, he steadily becomes an educated man, and is continually brought to the threshold of worship as his character becomes stronger and purer. It is well to remember that a man engaged upon shoddy work tends to develop a shoddy character unless he arms himself against it.

'Art,' we are told by men who have a title to speak, 'is in reality doing a good piece of work in the right way.' The dream of the artist is of a world in which there are many craftsmen pouring out upon the task under hand all their powers of honesty and sincerity. Thus, and thus only, were our great churches reared in a bygone day. The combined spirits of the craftsmen supported the pure minds of the divinely inspired architects who, as they pondered and meditated, designed the imperishable homes of God. No great architecture symbolizing man's worship can ever be born of an industrial system subordinated to mere financial profit. It is no more right to worship the golden calf in England than it was for the Israelites at the foot of Sinai.

EDUCATION AND KNOWLEDGE

Working men and women will be drawn irresistibly back to worship God in our churches when Christians seek not only to talk and persuade, but also to plan their own lives simply in accordance with the divine principle of renunciation. The forces they would free by doing this would rapidly bring order into the confused welter of modern life and increase the number of those unhindered in the expression of their powers. Education would advance by leaps and bounds and knowledge would not only increase, but be rightly used. Some people confuse education and knowledge. The latter is the instrument of the former. The more knowledge a man has the wiser he needs to be, so that he may use it for good and not ill.

Knowledge in the possession of a rogue is as a jemmy in the hands of a burglar. In the hands of a fool it is as a razor in the hands of a baby. In spite of this there are those who would seek to divorce spiritual things from our schools. The truth is that worship, education, and knowledge are as three strands in a triple cord not quickly broken.

As England sets herself to give the maximum of education to her children, as she will be driven to do after the Great War, she must remember that the nation that seeks to rely upon the development of mind and body alone, forgetting the things of the spirit, will infallibly bring ruin not only to herself, but to the nations around.

In ordinary life the merely clever man is as detestable as he is able. Knowledge can serve a man for a time, but only worship can bring its service to abiding value. Out of worship springs all that is good in our common life.

The Need of Worship

As a man worships he opens his spirit and consequently his body and mind to the things which are infinite and eternal. He stands on the boundaries of known things and gazes into the face of God as revealed to him in the perfect beauty of Christ. With his fellows he kneels before the altar of God and in the highest moments of corporate worship partakes of the Blessed Sacrament of the body and blood of Christ, which will sustain him, whatever chances or toils may be set in his life.

Now let us speak more directly.

If you are oppressed by toil and the injustice of men, do not make the mistake of deeming such things a full excuse for drifting with the current of the world. Turn your face to Christ, claim your right to a place in His Church, even if some people give you a cold welcome there, for He will welcome you and lift you up with new courage and strength.

If you are educated in the ordinary sense of the word, and are contented with the satisfaction of the mind, still you must worship something or somebody! Is it fame, or riches, or power, or humanity? There is only One who abides for ever; all other things are the shadows of His motion. To be content with shadows is to have missed the true goal of education.

If you worship God in His Church, sooner or later you will know that you must bring before the altar, as a living sacrifice, your body with its capacities of service, and your mind stored with all attainable knowledge. A Christian man who neglects his own mind is not offering to God the best that he is meant to give. Moreover, it is only the men who worship who can prevent human knowledge from ministering to corruption or destruction, and instead make it the instrument of healing and service to humanity.

5. CHURCH TUTORIAL CLASSES

(The Church Tutorial Classes Association is a comparatively recent foundation. Yet as early as June 1917 the following article appeared in the *Church Quarterly Review*. In the main it outlines a proposal for the further education of adult church men and women. In the light of the tract written in 1916 for the Society for Promoting Christian Knowledge the proposal is interesting. The article rapidly surveys the progress and freedom of University Tutorial Classes, and shows their great effect upon the serious study of members of various churches.)

IT is probable that the purest results of educational effort are secured in response to the simple demands of quite ordinary people, and although the development of a national system of education is, and must always be, essential, yet it is clear that greater effort is necessary in connection with it to secure a proportionate return than would be the case when unorganized demand finds expression and is satisfied outside the area of the system.

It seems that, if we would make new discoveries in education, we must contemplate fundamental human needs long and carefully.

The area of what we may term the education of children and adolescents is well occupied. There are experts in every county and considerable town apart from the large numbers of people who occupy their time in teaching. Systematization is the order of the day, and it is noteworthy that all proposals for reform which have been recently accepted by representative bodies are concerned with the importance of the existing system rather than with what is so desirable— the opening up of fresh methods, even, it may be, to the point of revolution.

So far as the system is concerned, there is little freedom for educational experiment except in favoured places in the universities, but their area, and especially that part of it commonly known to the public, is mainly occupied by students continuing their education and, in that aspect, conforms, and tends still further to conform, to the national educational system.

The question as to whether all adults should be systematically educated is a difficult one to answer, but it is quite certain that there will never be any attempt to force adult men and women into one type of educational institution in the same way that boys and girls of diverse capacities have been forced into schools which were originally, and should in large measure always be, training places for scholarship.

Directly any successful piece of educational work affecting the adult community realizes itself, however, the system seeks to absorb it, and this for two reasons—one, because every educational authority is anxious to extend its influence, and the other because such educational efforts seek the financial assistance of the State. A close observer of the development of the University Extension movement can trace both these tendencies steadily at work, but it is more marked in regard to the University Tutorial Class movement, which has secured substantial financial aid from the State through the Board of Education and, within less than ten years, has found a prominent place within the system of national education. At the same time the regulations which hedge it about were rightly formed to fit the classes rather than the classes to fit the regulations, the latter of which methods so often prevails when educational experts get to work.

The University Tutorial Class is a rediscovery by working men and women of the method of Plato. It makes no claim to novelty, but it has utilized the characteristics of the mature mind and has harmonized with them. It could not do otherwise because the class was conceived in the first place by a group of working men and women who, for the sake of development and the delight of learning, were ready to devote their entire leisure for a long period to combined study. Naturally enough, the subjects in which they were interested were such as affected their everyday life—the conditions of the development of the community in which they lived, the evolution of, and the position occupied by, their own work in particular and by labour in general. With a sure instinct they overthrew the idea of being taught in the sense that even an undergraduate is taught, because, full of self-respect tempered by humility, they knew that no teacher who had learnt merely from books could place before them the whole of an argument concerning industrial or social life. They were keen to learn not only from the teacher, but from one another. Without any illusory ideas as to the strenuousness of the labours they proposed, they pledged themselves to study for three years, not missing an attendance unless compelled, to read as much as they could in their limited time, and to write essays regularly; but they stipulated for that freedom which is essential in all adult education, the freedom which allows the most unlearned to teach without fear, and the most learned to listen not merely with patience but with gratitude.

It would almost seem that such groups of adults would become loose and unimportant institutions, but that is far from the case. Because of the keenness of the students, and partly because of their powerful minds steeled by labour, the educational results achieved are striking, so much so that there has never been any doubt that the work done may be considered to be on the level of honours work in the university. Moreover, the finest teachers of our time have been not only glad but anxious to teach these classes, affirming almost without exception that they too are learners in them.

The classes are attached to every university and university college in England and Wales. Four years ago they began to spread in the dominions, and are at work in connection with the six universities of Australia and the three university colleges of New Zealand, whilst beginnings have been made in both Canada and South Africa. The war, with all its disastrous effects, although it has reduced the number of the classes, has left the whole system intact and, in some parts where conditions are favourable, the number of classes has increased.

The story of the development of these classes is assuredly romantic. It is full of sacrifice and of devotion. 'It is a revelation of the soul of a people.'[1] It has been described as 'the most important development in the history of British education since the Act of 1870.'[2] It may be read in detail

[1] *Glasgow Herald.*   [2] *Hibbert Journal.*

in the volume *University Tutorial Classes : a Study in the Development of Higher Education among Working Men and Women.*[1]

Quite early in the movement the attention of leaders of the churches was drawn to the necessity for similar work in their various communions, and, although there are few definite records of the establishment of such classes, yet the fact that the Tutorial Classes for general education have existed has had a marked effect on the development of serious study among the members of the various churches.

Actual efforts have been made in the Church of England. Classes which have attained a real degree of success have been established more or less on experimental lines. A report was made to a recent meeting of theological college principals on a successful class at Leeds. Tentative efforts were also reported at Liverpool. The idea that these classes should operate in connection with the men and women of the Church of England gives rise to many fruitful suggestions. They would tend to raise the level of education in the Church, not only amongst the laity but amongst the clergy. They would provide a real contribution towards the solution of the hitherto insoluble problem of drawing men of varied experiences to the ministry of the Church. But, above all, they would make it clear that the finest fruits of the mind are a fitting sacrifice for all Christians to make. Not indeed that all the laity, or even all the clergy, should become scholars, but those who have the gifts of scholarship should exercise them to the full. If the Church needs any temporal possession at all it surely is the possession of knowledge. There should be no rest on the part of her members until the fullness of learning is within her courts. In quite an ordinary way members of the Church in their place and degree should have clear ideas of the central truths of the faith, and should know something of the story of the years, and have power to connect all this with the general knowledge of the time which must be utilized for the mission of the Church. This cannot be general unless a certain proportion are reaching out untiringly and

[1] Longmans, Green & Co.

c

unceasingly for knowledge which will illumine the whole mind of the Church.

Proposals for the definite establishment of classes have been considered more seriously in the diocese of Southwark than elsewhere, and a committee instructed to take steps to establish classes in the diocese is at work under the authorization of the Diocesan Conference and of the bishop. Much of the detail will have to be decided upon as the result of experiment, because no system can be imposed upon adult minds for more than a limited period, but certain things are clear and, of these, the most outstanding are:

(1) That such classes shall be, roughly speaking, of a university level, and to secure this they shall be attached to the theological faculties in universities or to theological colleges; thus no teacher will be approved other than by such authority.

(2) That the classes shall operate for a prolonged period and shall aim at giving a complete education within the limitations of the subject studied; that the subjects, whatever they be, shall be studied from a distinctly Christian point of view; in a word, they shall be in the best sense propagandist.

(3) They shall be administered as far as possible by committees representing both the students and the teachers.

Most of these ideas are gained from the experience of the University Tutorial Class movement. The connection with theological colleges would be most fruitful because it would be possible to make provision for summer schools, and even for retreats. Just as universities have gained, so they would gain by striking their roots deep into the adult population. It is not proposed that their staffs should teach, other than at summer schools, except where it was both desirable and possible, but they should authorize teachers whom they would be willing to utilize should occasion arise.

Although it is not proposed that the classes should form a course of preparation for holy orders, yet it is obvious that men who joined them, even whilst they were engaged in field, factory, or workshop, would receive a real measure of education which would enable them, if called to the ministry of the

Church, to pursue their subsequent training with certain hope of success. It must not be forgotten that a student who had been in a class for a prolonged period pursuing his studies would stand completely revealed so far as character and ability were concerned. He would have been brought to the knowledge of not merely the class, but the theological college, and probably the bishop.

As has already been said, the arrangement of details must await experiment. It would be interesting to attempt to discover the best time for the classes to be held, and how far they can be harmonized with the Sunday school and Bible class system of the Church. Some may think that the Church Tutorial Class should be at the summit of every complete Sunday school system, so that the child might have the opportunity to go step by step until in the Tutorial Class he, or she, reaches the area of the influence of the theological college. On the other hand, it might be better for the classes to be entirely detached. Even now in the University Tutorial Class system matters of detail are left to the individual classes; much more must it be so at the beginning of Church Tutorial Classes.

It is not necessary to develop a plea for study to any greater extent than has already been done. The purpose which can best be achieved is to draw the attention of church men and women to an experiment which in some form or other must assuredly be undertaken if the Church is to do her perfect work in a time of extraordinary difficulty.

There is no reason why Church Tutorial Classes should not be established anywhere. If working men and women will study for long periods without hope of reward (and they have discarded all offers of diplomas and certificates) for the glory of citizenship, it is certain that, even though reluctant church men and women be included, there are numbers who, the plain duty set before them, will study for the glory of God and the extension of His Kingdom on earth. There is no reason why in any group of parishes a meeting should not be summoned, if ten or more students are ready to pledge themselves and know what they want to study, and the detailed plan considered. It should not be difficult to find a teacher and, by so doing, many a scholar clergyman, isolated as he may easily be, will find new hope in the exercise of his own peculiar gift.

Isolated effort increases in strength when it is linked to other efforts. The necessary links can be made for the present through the medium of the committee of the diocese of Southwark, which has suggested the formation of a national committee which will be called together in the near future.

The formation of the classes, or their equivalent, is so important that the weakest demand cannot be allowed to die down for the want of ready and efficient help. Central sources, whether in regard to books, or teachers, or organization, will of necessity form themselves immediately.

Finally, the general ferment in education which is rising in the whole country must find its expression in the ranks of the Church of God.

If the suggestions made here are not adequate to the pressing need, it is the immediate and plain duty of members of the Church to bestir themselves, and to decide how and in what manner they can develop for the glory of God the powers that lie hidden in their minds.

6. CITIZENSHIP

(In August 1917 this article appeared as Chapter V of *Cambridge Essays on Education*, which was edited by A. C. Benson and published by Cambridge University Press. Citizenship is here described as 'the art of living together on the highest plane of human life.' It is very necessary that schools should give a training in citizenship; as to whether such training should consist of direct teaching, in addition to, or apart from, the communal spirit, is a controversial point, and is here discussed at some length. The development of civics, from the point of view of education, in America and England, up to 1917, is reviewed in detail.)

I. Direct Training for Citizenship

THERE is no institution in national life which can free itself from the responsibility of training for citizenship those who come under its influence, whether they be men or women. The problem is common to all institutions, although it may present itself in diverse forms appropriate to varying ages and experiences. It is primarily the problem of all schools and places of education.

The aim of education, according to Comenius, is 'to train generally all who are born to all that is human.' From that definition it follows that the purpose of any school must be to bear its part in developing to the utmost the powers of body, mind, and spirit for the common good. It must be to secure the application of the finest attributes of the race to the work of developing citizenship, which is the art of living together on the highest plane of human life.

Citizenship is, in reality, the focusing point of all human virtues, though it is often illuminated by the consciousness of a city not made with hands. It represents in a practical form the spirit of courage, unselfishness, and sympathy consecrated to service in time of war and peace. Generally speaking, in England and her dominions, citizenship is developed in harmony with an ideal of democracy.

The progress of democracy is irresistible [says de Tocqueville], because it is the most uniform, the most ancient, and the most permanent tendency to be found in history.

But its right working is dependent entirely upon uplift,

not only of mind, but of spirit. The democratic community, above all other communities, must have within itself schools which at one and the same time impart information concerning the theory and methods of its government and inspire consecration to social service rather than to individual welfare, schools which reveal the transcendence of the interests of the State as compared with the interests of any individual or group of individuals within it. The democratic state has been compared to 'one huge Christian personality, one mighty growth or stature of an honest man.' Out of this comparison arises the idea of citizenship reaching out beyond the boundaries of a single state—one honest man among many—and thus responsibility is placed upon the schools to develop knowledge of, and sympathy with, the activities and aspirations of human life in many nations. The comity of nations depends directly upon the intellectual and spiritual honesty which obtains in each of them, and true strength of nationality arises more from the exercise of these qualities than from extent of area or of productive power.

Every subject taught in a school should serve the needs of the larger citizenship; if it fails to do so it is either wrongly taught or superfluous.

Social welfare depends upon the right use of knowledge by the individual, however restricted or developed that knowledge may be, whether it be acquired in elementary school or university.

There has been much discussion concerning the relative importance of the development of community spirit in the schools and the introduction of the direct teaching of citizenship. The methods are not mutually exclusive; their operations are distinct. The school which does not develop community spirit, which does not fit into its place in the work of training the complete man, is obviously imperfect. The same cannot be said of the school which does not provide direct instruction in citizenship; for teaching may be given in so many indirect ways. Some consideration of what has happened in this connection both in England and America will perhaps be most helpful, although the intangible nature of the results would render dangerous any attempt to make definite pronouncements on their success or failure.

Largely as the result of the realization of the immediate relationship between national education and national productivity there are abundant signs that the English educational system is about to be developed. The ordinary argument has been well put:

A new national spirit has been aroused in our people by the war; if we are to recover and improve our position at the end of the war that national spirit must be maintained; for unless every man and woman comes to know and feel that industry, agriculture, commerce, shipping, and credit are national concerns, and that education is a potent means for the promotion of these objects among others, we shall fail in the great effort of national recuperation. In plainer words, our great firms will not make money, wages will fall, and wage-earners will be out of work.[1]

The possibility of the extension of the educational system to meet the needs of technical training need not cause disquiet among those whose desire is for fullness of citizenship, if they are prepared to insist that teachers shall be trained on broad and comprehensive lines, and that every vocational course shall include instruction in direct citizenship. The argument is ready to hand and simple. If all men and women must strive to work wisely and well, so also should they learn how to participate in the government, local and national, which their work supports. Moreover, the right study of a trade or profession induces a perception of the interrelationship of all human activity.

On the other hand it is important that vocational work, at least so far as it is carried out by manual training, should be introduced into schemes of liberal education. In this connection it is worth recalling that in a recent report the Consultative Committee of the Board of Education expressed with complete conviction the opinion that manual training was indispensable in places of secondary education:

We consider that our secondary education has been too exclusively concerned with the cultivation of the mind by means of books and the instruction of the teacher. To this essential aim there must be added as a condition of balance and completeness that of fostering those qualities of mind and that skill of hand which are evoked by systematic work.

[1] *Interim Report of the Consultative Committee of the Board of Education on Scholarships for Higher Education*, May 1916.

In this way would be generated that 'sympathetic and understanding contact between all brain workers and the complete men who work with both hands and brain' so strongly pleaded for by Professor Lethaby, who insists that 'some teaching about the service of labour must be got into all our educational schemes.'

It must be remembered that the question of vocational training affects chiefly the proposed system of compulsory continuation school education up to the age of eighteen, which has yet to be established for all boys and girls not in attendance at secondary schools or who have not completed a satisfactory period of attendance.[1]

The inadequacy of the period of education allotted to the vast mass of the population and the need for educational reform in many directions can only be noted; both these matters, however, affect citizenship profoundly.

It is upon the expectation of early development on the following lines, indicated without detail, that our consideration of the possibilities of schools in regard to citizenship must be based:

(1) A longer period of elementary school life during which no child shall be employed for other than educational purposes.

(2) The establishment of compulsory continuation schools for all boys and girls up to the age of eighteen, the hours of attendance to be allowed out of reasonable working hours.

(3) Complete opportunity for qualified boys and girls to continue their technical or humane studies from the elementary school to the university.

(4) A distinct improvement in the supply and power of teachers, chiefly as the result of better training in connection with universities and the establishment of a remuneration which will enable them to live in the manner demanded by the nature and responsibilities of their calling.

The two main aspects of the development of citizenship

---

[1] See Final Report of the Departmental Committee on Juvenile Education in Relation to Employment after the War, 1917, Cd. 8512. The Bill 'to make further provision with respect to Education in England and Wales and for purposes connected therewith' (Bill 89) had not been introduced by Mr. Fisher when this article was written.

through the schools which have already been noted may be summarized as follows, and may be considered separately:

(1) The direct teaching of civics or of citizenship.

(2) The development through the ordinary school community of the qualities of the good citizen.

The Direct Study of Citizenship

The study in schools of civic relations has been developed to a much greater extent in America than in England. This is probably due largely to the fact that the American need is the more obvious. In normal times there is a constant influx of people of different nationalities to the United States whom it is the aim of the Government to make into American citizens. At the same time there is in America a greater disposition than in England to adapt abstract study to practical ends, to link the class-room to the factory, to the city hall, and to the Capitol itself. As one of her scholars says:

Both the inspiration and the romance of the scholar's life lie in the perfect assurance that any truth, however remote or isolated, has its part in the unity of the world of truth and its undreamed-of applicability to service.[1]

There are in America numerous societies, among them the National Education Association, the American Historical Association, the National Municipal League, the American Political Science Association, which are working steadily to make the study of civics an essential feature of every part of the educational system. Their prime purposes are summarized as follows:

(1) To awaken a knowledge of the fact that the citizen is in a social environment whose laws bind him for his own good.

(2) To acquaint the citizen with the forms of organization and methods of administration of government in its several departments.[2]

They claim that this can best be done by means of bringing the young citizen into direct contact with the significant facts of the life of his own local community and of the national community. To indicate this more clearly they have applied to the study the name of 'Community Civics.'

[1] Peabody, *The Religion of an Educated Man.*
[2] Haines, *The Teaching of Government.*

* c

The argument that a sense of unreality may arise as a result of the apparent completeness of knowledge gained in the school is met by the close contact maintained all the time with the community outside.

There is unanimity of opinion that civics shall be taught from the elementary school onwards.

We believe [runs the report of the Committee of Eight of the American Historical Association] that elementary civics should permeate the entire school life of the child.   In the early grades the most effective features of this instruction will be directly connected with the teaching of regular subjects in the course of study.   Through story, poem, and song there is the quickening of those emotions which influence civic life.   The works and biographies of great men furnish many opportunities for incidental instruction in civics.   The elements of geography serve to emphasize the interdependence of men—the very earliest lesson in civic instruction.   A study of pictures and architecture arouses the desire for civic beauty and orderliness. [1]

A recent inquiry by a committee of the American Political Science Association makes it quite clear that the subject is actually taught in the bulk of the elementary and secondary schools of the various states and that generally the results are satisfactory, or indicate clearly necessary reforms.   The difficulty of providing suitable text-books is partly met by the addition of supplementary local information.

There are very few colleges and universities which do not provide courses in political science.

No claim is made that the teaching of civics makes of necessity good citizens, but merely that it makes the good citizen into a better one.   The justification of the subject lies in its own content.

It is a study of an important phase of human society and, for this reason, has the same value as elementary science or history. [2]

There is, moreover, throughout the various American reports, an insistence on the power of the community ideal in the school and the necessity for discipline in the performance of school duties and a due appreciation of the importance of individual action in relation to the class and to the school.

In England there has been much general and unco-ordinated

---

[1] Haines, *The Teaching of Government.*

[2] Bourne, *The Teaching of History and Civics in the Elementary and Secondary School.*

advocacy of the direct teaching of citizenship, but, for various reasons, it does not appear to have been introduced generally into the schools, nor does there appear to be any immediate likelihood of development in the existing schools.

The Civic and Moral Education League made definite inquiry, in 1915, of teachers and schools. They pronounced the results to be disappointing, though they comforted themselves with the incontrovertible dictum that 'the people who are doing most have least time to talk about it.' As the result of their inquiry, they drew up a statement of the aims of civics which in general and in detail differed little from the ideas accepted in America.

If compulsory continued education is introduced for boys and girls who now have no school education after the elementary school, it is of the utmost importance that the direct study should be included in some form or other before the age of eighteen is reached, and it is in connection with this type of school rather than in connection with the elementary or secondary school that constructive efforts should be made.

It must be remembered that Mr. Acland, when Minister for Education, introduced the subject into the Elementary Code of 1895, and provided a detailed syllabus. This was generally approved, not only as the action of a progressive administrator, but as an evidence of the new spirit of freedom beginning to reveal itself in the educational system.

There are some education authorities, like the County of Chester, which enact that the study of citizenship shall proceed side by side with religious education, but the majority leave it to the teachers to do all that is necessary by the adaptation of other subjects and the development of school spirit.

The elaborate nature of Mr. Acland's syllabus tended to defeat its object, and some held it to be psychologically unsound, but there has also been lack of suitable text-books. In general, however, the whole subject depends peculiarly upon the personality of the teacher who feels no lack of text-books if he is alive to the interest of his lesson.

In *Studies on Board Schools*[1] there is a delightful study of a

[1] Charles Morley, 1897.

lesson on 'Rates' to young citizens with the altruistic text, 'All for Each, Each for All.' 'Citizen Carrots,' a tired newspaper boy up every morning at five, is revealed as responding with great enthusiasm to this interesting lesson, which commences with a drawing on a blackboard of a 'regulation workhouse, a board school, a free library, a lamp post, a water cart, a dustman, a policeman, a steam roller, a navvy or two, and a long-handled shovel stuck in a heap of soil.' A hypothetical payer of rates, 'Mrs. Smith,' is revealed as getting a great deal for her rates:

She is protected from any harm; her property is safe; she can walk about the streets with comfort by day or night; her drains are seen to; her rubbish is taken away for her; she has books and newspapers to read; if she has ten children she can have them well taught for nothing—so that if they are willing to learn, and attend school regularly, they can very easily make their own living when they grow up; if she is ill, she can go to the infirmary for medicine; and if, when she grows old, she is unable to pay rent or buy food or clothes, these things are provided for her.

'And please, sir, the parks,' interjected the eager Carrots.

If the definition of a good citizen propounded by Professor Masterman is true—that he is one who pays his rates without grumbling — 'Citizen Carrots,' whatever his disadvantages, is intellectually anyhow on the way to become such a citizen, and certainly in the sketch 'Citizen Carrots' is determined that the rates shall be expended properly because he himself will have a vote in later days.

It is probable that lessons such as these are more frequent than the time-tables would indicate. There are few headmasters of elementary schools who would disclaim the adequate teaching of citizenship in their schools. They would explain that the treatment of history and geography proceeding from local standpoints was effective in this direction, and it is the rule rather than otherwise for visits to be paid to places of historic interest within reach of the schools. Advantage is also taken of such days as Empire Day to stimulate interest in the State, as well as to impart knowledge concerning its organization. All this is reinforced by the use of appropriate reading books which are instruments of indirect, but not necessarily less effective, instruction.

The larger opportunities which secondary schools offer have not been taken advantage of to induce the specific study of civics to any greater extent than in the elementary schools, although many schools are able to devote at least a period each week to the consideration of current events, and, naturally, the teaching of history and geography includes much more completely the consideration of institutions both at home and abroad.

The idea of the regional or local survey is gaining ground, and in some respects it will prove to serve the same purpose as the 'Community Civics' of the American High School.

There have been attempts to introduce economics into the secondary school curriculum, but they have not persisted to any extent. In the *Memorandum on Curricula of Secondary Schools*, issued by the Board of Education in 1913, it is suggested that

It will sometimes be desirable to provide, for those who propose on leaving school to enter business, a special commercial course with special study of the more technical side of economic theory and some study of political and constitutional history.

For the rest there is no mention of the subjects intimately connected with government. It is clear that the Board expects that out of the subjects of the ordinary curriculum, with such special efforts suggested by public interest as may from time to time occur, the student will gain a general knowledge of the affairs of the community round about, some knowledge of the principles of politics, clear ideas concerning movements for social reform, and some acquaintance with international problems. If he does so he will have secured a useful introduction to the studies associated with adult life.

An intelligent study of languages will help materially in this direction and, whilst this is specially true in the cases of Greek and Latin, there is no reason why modern languages should not serve the same purpose. It is, however, often the case that the study of the history and institutions of modern countries is not associated sufficiently with the study of their language.

The public and grammar schools of England, as contrasted

with the newer secondary schools, are more especially the homes of classical studies, and it is through the working of these schools that the knowledge of institutions in ancient Greece and Rome will have its greatest effect on citizenship.

The study of political science as a specific subject is gaining ground in universities, whilst the study of the empire and its institutions has naturally made rapid progress during the last few years. There may also be noted distinct tendencies, arising out of the experience of the war, towards the foundation of schools destined to deal with the institutions and the thought of foreign countries. In the schools of economics and history there is fullness of attempt to study all that can be included under the generic title of civics, which, after all, may be defined as political and social science interpreted in immediate and practical ways.

II. INDIRECT TRAINING FOR CITIZENSHIP

After all is said and done the ideal training for citizenship in the schools depends more upon the wisdom engendered in the pupil than upon the direct study of civics. If the spirits of men and women are set in a right direction they will reach out for knowledge as for hid treasure. 'Wisdom is more moving than any motion; she passeth and goeth through all things by reason of her pureness.'[1]

It happens also in natural sequence that the spirit developed in a school will lead to the construction of institutions in connection with school life calculated to secure its adequate expression.

Elementary schools, however, are much handicapped in this way. If it comes about that work other than educational or recreative is forbidden to children during the years of attendance at school, and also that the period of school life is lengthened, there will be opportunity for the development of games on a self-governing basis. Elementary school children have a large measure of initiative; all they need is a real chance to exercise it. They would willingly make their schools real

---

[1] Wisdom of Solomon, vii. 24.

centres of child life. Many children at present have little else than narrow tenements and the streets, out of which influences arise which war continually against the social influences of the school.

The opportunity afforded by well-ordered leisure would be accentuated by the more complete operation of movements, such as boys' brigades, boy scouts, girl guides, and church lads' brigades, which are in their several ways doing much to develop citizenship. Such bodies are now in effect educational authorities, and classes are organized by them in connection with the Board of Education.

There have been many attempts to introduce self-governing experiments into elementary schools and, whilst they have often been defeated by reason of the immaturity of the children, yet some of them have met with great success. The election of monitors on the lines of a general election is an instance of success in this direction. The ideas which have arisen from the advocacy of the Montessori system have induced methods of greater freedom in connection with many aspects of elementary school life. The Caldecott Community, dealing with working-class children in the neighbourhood of St. Pancras, has tried many interesting experiments. That, however, of the introduction of children's courts of justice had to be abandoned, but not until many valuable lessons in child psychology had been learnt.

Side by side with the elementary school there are rising in England experiments similar to those undertaken by such organizations as the school city and the George Junior Republics of America. The most notable among them is the Little Commonwealth, Dorchester, which has achieved astonishing results through the process of taking delinquent children and allowing them self-government. But, hopeful as the prospects are, their ultimate effect will be best estimated when their pupils, restored in youth to the honourable service of the community, are taking their full share in life as adult citizens, and naturally every care is taken in the organization of these institutions to ensure that the transition from their sheltered citizenship to the outside world shall not be of so abrupt a nature as to tend to render unreal and remote the life in which the children have taken part.

Nearly all of the more recent experiments in regard to the school and its kindred institutions are co-operative in principle and in method, but it is probably Utopian to conceive an educational method which shall achieve the highest success without having included within it the element of competition. If competition is a method obtaining outside the school it is bound to reproduce itself within it. The only possible thing for the school to do is to restrict the influence of competition to the channels where it can be beneficial.

The method by which elementary school children pass to the secondary school is by means of competitive scholarships. In common with the Consultative Committee of the Board of Education it is necessary to accept the fact that at present 'the scholarship system is too firmly rooted in the manner, habits, and character of this country to be dislodged, even if it were thrice condemned by theory.'[1] But, in the interests of citizenship, scholarships should be awarded as the result of non-competitive tests, if only to secure that every child shall receive the education for which he or she is fitted.

The stress and strain imposed upon many who climb the ladder of education, often occasioned by the inadequacy of the scholarship for the purposes to which it is to be applied, tend to develop characteristics which are so strongly individual as to be distinctly anti-social.

It is unfortunate that in many subjects of the curriculum it is not merely bad form to help one's neighbour, but distinctly a school sin, and this makes it necessary for a balance to be struck by the introduction of subjects at which all can work for the good of the class or the school. Manual work and local surveys are subjects of this nature, and should be encouraged side by side with games of which there are three essential aspects: the individual achievement, the winning of the match or race, and 'playing the game.' In reference to citizenship the last of these is the only one which ultimately matters.

[1] *Interim Report of the Consultative Committee of the Board of Education on Scholarships for Higher Education,* 1916.

It is generally admitted that the great public schools are those which are most characteristic of English boy life at its best. Glorying as they do in a splendid tradition, they have always had in addition the opportunity of adapting themselves to new needs. Their reform is always under discussion and perchance they are waiting even now for some Arnold or Thring to lead them in a new England, for new it will inevitably be. Even so, the sense of responsibility they have developed has been translated into the terms of English government over half the world.

The objective of the public school boy anxious to take a part in government at home has always been Parliament, or such local institutions as demand his service in accordance with the tradition of his family. The tendency to despise the homely duties of a city councillor or poor law guardian is, however, passing. There are few schools which do not welcome visitors to speak to the boys who have first-hand acquaintance with the life of the poor, or who are indeed of that life themselves. In this way boys get to realize, as far as it is possible through sympathy, what it means to be out of work, what it means to be hungry for unattainable learning, what children have to suffer, and, in addition to the practical interest which many boys immediately develop, it cannot be doubted that many ideals for the conduct of social life in the future are conceived, even if dimly, for the first time. Thanks to the unremitting efforts of large-minded headmasters, public school boys more and more realize that they are beneficiaries of the spirit of a past day, not only in the sense of the creation of a noble tradition, but actually in regard to the material provision of buildings and the financial support of teaching.

There is likely to be an extension of university education in the near future. The ancient universities of Oxford and Cambridge, with their great college system, will be strengthened, as will be the universities which were established at the end of the nineteenth and the beginning of the twentieth century. The demand for the better training of teachers will result inevitably in the creation of more universities. The inadequate sum which this country has spent upon university education up to the present will be greatly increased.

As a direct result of the opportunity which university life gives to undergraduates for the development of self-governing institutions, there can be little doubt that the university must be regarded above all other schools and most institutions as powerful in the development of good citizenship. The public school tradition will be carried directly into the older universities, and in increasing measure into the new universities as the best spirit of the public schools gradually permeates the whole system of our education even down to the elementary schools themselves. When these opportunities so lavishly provided for the development of student life in its self-governing aspects are realized, and when above it all there stand great teachers in the lineage of those described by Cardinal Newman in his eulogy of Athens—'the very presence of Plato,' to the student, 'a stay for his mind to rest on, a burning thought in his heart, a bond of union with men like himself, ever afterwards'—little else can be desired. In every university there must be such teachers, or universities will tend to fall to the level of the life about them. 'You can infuse,' said Lord Rosebery at the Congress of the Universities of the Empire, 'character, and morals, and energy, and patriotism by the tone and atmosphere of your university and your professors.'

From one point of view all the old universities of Europe—Bologna, Paris, Prague, Oxford, Cambridge, etc.—must be regarded as definite and conscious protests against the dividing and isolating—the anti-civic—forces of the periods of their institution. They represent historically the development of communities for common interest and protection in the great and holy cause of the pursuit of learning, and, above all things, their story is the story of the growth of European unity and citizenship.

The feudal and ecclesiastical order of the old medieval world were both alike threatened by the power that had so strangely sprung up in the midst of them. Feudalism rested on local isolation, on the severance of kingdom from kingdom and barony from barony, on the distinction of blood and race, on the supremacy of material or brute force, on an allegiance determined by accidents of place and social position. The university, on the other hand, was a protest against this isolation of man from man. The smallest school was European and not local.[1]

The spirit which is characteristic of a university in its best aspects, linked with the spirit which is inherent in the ranks of working people, has on more occasions than one set on foot movements for the education of the people. One of the most notable instances of this unity found expression at the Oxford Co-operative Congress of 1882, when Arnold Toynbee urged co-operators to undertake the education of the citizen. By this he meant 'the education of each member of the community as regards the relation in which he stands to other individual citizens and to the community as a whole.' 'We have abandoned,' he said further, 'and rightly abandoned the attempt to realize citizenship by separating ourselves from society. We will never abandon the belief that it has yet to be won amid the stress and confusion of the ordinary world in which we move.' From that day to this co-operators have always had before them an ideal of education in citizenship, and have organized definite teaching year by year.

Another instance of even greater power lies in the co-operation between the pioneers of the University Extension movement at Cambridge and the working men, particularly of Rochdale and Nottingham, to be followed later by that unprecedented revival of learning amongst working people which took place in Northumberland and Durham in the days before the great coal strike. At a later date, in 1903, the same kind of united action gave rise to the movement of the Workers' Educational Association, which has always conceived its purpose to be the development of citizenship in and through education pursued in common by university man and working man alike. The system of University Tutorial Classes originated by this association has been based upon an ideal of citizenship, and not primarily upon a determination to acquire knowledge, although it was clearly seen that vague aspirations towards good citizenship without the harnessing of all available knowledge to its cause would be futile. After exception has been made for the body of young men and women who are

[1] J. R. Green, *A Short History of the English People*.

determined to acquire technical education for the laudable purpose of advancing both their position in life and their utility to society, it is clear that no educational appeal to working men and women will have the least effect if it is not directed towards the purpose of enriching their life, and through them the life of the community. The proof of this lies in the fact that, after they have striven together for years in Tutorial Classes, they ask for no recognition—in fact they have declined it when it has been offered—and have devoted their powers to voluntary civic work and the work of the associations or unions to which they belong, as well as, in very many instances, to the spreading of education throughout the districts in which they live. It is largely due to the leaven of educational enthusiasm which has thus been generated that there is a unanimous movement on the part of working people towards a complete educational system including within it compulsory attendance at continuation schools during the day.

The problems that hedge about continuation schools are many, but it is clear that they will be regarded by educationists and by at least some employers as above all else training for citizenship based upon the vocation to which the boy or girl may be devoting himself or herself in working hours. The narrowness of the daily occupation, divorced as it is from the whole spirit and intent of apprenticeship, will be broadened directly the consideration of daily work is placed in the continuation school both on a higher plane and in a complete setting.

The compulsory evening school will fail unless it induces a demand for recreation of a pure kind which may be associated with the voluntary evening school and continued along the lines of study into the years of adult life. And even if it is impossible for every student of capacity in the continuation school to pass into the university or technological college, it may be hoped that there need not fail to be opportunities for reaching the heights of ascertained knowledge in the University Tutorial Class. In the future, as now, only in greater degree, such classes will be regarded as an essential part of university work, and will provide opportunity for the study of those subjects which are most nearly related to citizenship.

It is one of the fundamental principles of the Workers' Educational Association that every person, when not under the power of some hostile overmastering influence, is ready to respond to an educational appeal. Not indeed that all are ready or able to become scholars, but that all are anxious to look with understanding eyes at the things which are pure and beautiful. Tired men and women are made better citizens if they are taken, as they often are, to picture galleries and museums, to places of historic interest and of scenic beauty, and are helped to understand them by the power of a sympathetic guide. It is by the extension of work of this sort, which can be carried out almost to a limitless extent, that the true purpose of social reform will be best served. It is by such means that the press may be elevated, the level of the cinema raised, the efforts of the demagogue neutralized.

The Workers' Educational Association is based upon the work of the elementary school and of the associations of working people, notably the co-operative societies and trade unions. The democratic methods obtaining in those associations have themselves proved a valuable contribution to citizenship, and have determined the democratic nature of all adult education. The right and freedom of the student to study what he wishes finds its counterpart in the reasonable demand that man shall live out his life as he wills, provided it moves in a true direction and is in harmony with the needs and aspirations of his fellows.

It has seemed in this review of the relation of schools and places of education to the development of citizenship that the fact of the operation of social influences has been implicit at every point. In any case there is, and can be, no doubt that the school, whilst instant in its effect upon the mind of the time, is always being either hindered or helped by the conditions obtaining in the society in which it is set. The relations existing between society and school are revealed in a process of action and reaction. Wilhelm von Humboldt said that 'whatever we wish to see introduced into the life of a nation must first be introduced into its schools.' Among other things, it is necessary to develop in the schools an appreciation of all work that is necessary for human welfare. This is the crux of all effort towards citizenship through education. In the long run there can be no full citizenship unless there is fullness of intention to discover capacity and to develop it not for the individual but for the common good. This is primarily the task of an educational system. If a man is set to work for which he is not fitted, whether it be the work of a student or a miner, he is thwarted in his innate desire to attain to the full expression of his being in and through association with his fellow men, whereas, when a man is doing the right work, that for which he has capacity, he rejoices in his labour and strives continually to perfect it by development of all his powers. The exercise of good citizenship follows naturally as the inevitable result of a rightly developed life. It may not be the citizenship which is exercised by taking active and direct part in methods of government. The son of Sirach, meditating on the place of the craftsman, said:

All these trust to their hands: and every one is wise in his work. Without these cannot a city be inhabited . . . they will maintain the state of the world, and all their desire is in the work of their craft.[1]

The times are different, and the needs of people have changed, but the true test of a citizen may be more in the healthiness of dominating purpose than in the possession and satisfaction of a variety of desires. To 'maintain the state of the world' is no mean ambition.

If it is difficult for a man to become the good citizen when employed on work for which he is unfitted, it is even more difficult for the man to do so who is set to shoddy work or to work which damages the community.

The task laid upon the school is heavy, but it does not stand alone. The family and the Church are its natural allies in the modern State.

All alike will make mistakes, but, if they clearly set before them the intention to do their utmost to free the capacity of all for the accomplishment of the good of all, wisdom will increase, and many tragedies in life will be averted.

Thus lofty ideals have presented themselves, but they will

[1] Ecclesiasticus, xxxviii. 31–4.

secure universal admission apart from the immediate practical considerations which bulk so largely and often so falsely in the minds of men, and which are frequently suggested by limitations of finance and lack of faith in the all-sufficient power of wisdom.

It is in the consecration of a people to its highest ideals that the true city and the true State become realized on earth, and the measure of its consecration, in spite of all devices of teaching or training however wise, determines the true level of citizenship at any time in any place.

7. MEMBERS ONE OF ANOTHER

(This hitherto unpublished sermon was preached in Salisbury Cathedral in February 1918. Its main themes are the place of labour in the national life and in the Church of God. In the disturbed days of war, a striking appeal is made on behalf of labour. In order to obtain the honour due to labour, education is vitally necessary, provided its aim is spiritual.)

And whether one member suffer, all the members suffer with it ; or one member be honoured, all the members rejoice with it.   Now ye are the body of Christ.

1 Cor. xii. 26, 27.

AT a time full of anxious questioning, of strange events, and of changing standards, it is well to remind ourselves of the fundamental, indivisible unity of humanity. We are indeed 'members one of another,' created, projected, by the Spirit of the living God.

As St. Paul thought upon 'the church of God which is at Corinth, them that are sanctified in Christ Jesus, called to be saints, with all that in every place call upon the name of Jesus Christ our Lord, both theirs and ours,' his prophetic vision must have swept the ages, and he must have yearned, as we yearn, for the time when the unity of man, as man, shall rise to the fullness of its expression in 'the Church, the body of Christ,' for the time when all men shall be conscious of their dependence one upon the other and upon the risen Lord, in just as intimate a way as the hand of the human body is dependent upon the foot and as both are dependent upon the brain.

It is our purpose, this evening, to think for a whole of the Church in relation to national life, but we must pause at such a time as this to call to mind those vast masses of men and women outside our nation who also are of the 'body of Christ,' with whose sufferings we suffer, at whose honour we rejoice. The eternal unity of the spirit is unshaken even though the temporal disunity of the material body reveals itself in the long-drawn agony of war.   Especially do I think of Russia— 'Holy Russia,' as she has been affectionately called by those who have lived with her mystics and saints, and who have rejoiced in the simple piety of her common people. Let us pray, joining our prayers with all the prayers of that disrupted people, that the only unifying force in human life, even Christ Jesus our Lord, may be allowed to work His perfect will.

For the rest, we must confine ourselves to thoughts arising out of a consideration of the place of labour in the national life, and especially in the Church of God.

There is in Ecclesiasticus—the Wisdom of Jesus the son of Sirach—an interesting discussion of the place of labour in the manifold life of the community:

All these trust to their hands, and every one is wise in his work. Without these cannot a city be inhabited. . . . They shall not be found where parables are spoken. But they will maintain the state of the world.

When this mighty church was built, I imagine that those who wrought so beautifully in stone and wood did not 'sit high in the congregation,' but without their skilled labour there would have been no glorious building, unceasing expression, as it is, of human worship.

The work on the building of a great church is a type of democracy in action. For democracy depends not on the 'vote,' which, after all, is a mere symbol at best, but upon all men and women, in their several places, doing their own work unhindered with the full force of their bodies, minds, and spirits. With the full force—that is the condition. If any one, whether he hinders himself or is hindered by others, uses less, the life and work of the whole community suffers.

It is characteristic of our time that every one asks perfect wisdom of the community, and especially of those portions of it entrusted with government, forgetting that such a manifestation can only be when each single unit contributes its own full quota of wisdom according to its place and degree. Men turn to the Church and say: 'Justify your claims!' 'Prophesy!' 'Lead us to peace!' 'Reveal to us the thought of the Most High!' forgetting that she can only do so in all her power when all her members, and especially those who question, are living consecrated lives truly set in the membership of the body of Christ.

Wisdom comes only with much seeking, through much

suffering, and in long time. 'Oh! send her out of thy holy heavens and from the throne of thy glory.'

Labour—and when I use the term I mean it in the sense of manual work—has been so depressed, so lightly esteemed, so hindered, by both Church and State, that it has perhaps only here and there made its full contribution of mind and spirit to the wisdom of government or to the wisdom of worship. We have all been incredibly foolish in regard to it.

Just now its great material power in the prosecution of this war for liberty, for freedom, for true democracy, is recognized by every one. That labour should keep unfalteringly, cheerfully at work is regarded as essential to victory. But this is only an outward sign of the invisible truth that no nation can order itself aright unless it so exercises its industry as to draw from it the maximum of mental and spiritual power.

Labour has always been in its essence the sweetest, the most uniform of all human occupations. Yet, in our stupidity, we have thought it to be inferior and even degrading. Even when we have not been oppressors, we have stood by, sheltering behind some artificial economic doctrine, whilst the workers have been sacrificed on the altar of the false god of profit. We have hugged our comfort and our luxuries whilst our wisdom and power to worship have slowly ebbed away, and would have entirely passed but for the fact that perforce, in order to live, we did some things rightly.

Not one man but many have worked the long days through on wages insufficient to maintain healthy human life, with their self-respect slipping away from them.

I want to be quite fair. There are many employers who have done, and are doing, their utmost not only to use labour properly but to honour it, just indeed as there are many workmen who set about their daily task in the spirit of the true craftsman, but, when once a pure activity has been subordinated to other than its true purpose, its whole level falls, and those who take part in it are hindered and thwarted at every turn.

Labour has for its purpose the strength and glory of human life. It has been subordinated to productivity and profit, so the true employer finds himself pulled down by an array of prices and the so-called market, whilst the workman who would do his best finds little or no opportunity. He must often do inferior or bad work, or reduce his speed to a pace which, if it had not a motive, would be intolerable. Instead of co-operating in a democracy of labour, he finds himself willy-nilly taking part in an ignoble industrial war.

Remember, I am not now speaking of sweated labour, but of that which takes place even to-day in the ordinary factory or workshop. The days, I trust, are wholly past when we shall have opportunity to wear clothes made at the price of the ebbing life and strength of innumerable women. I cannot think that English greed is wholly responsible for the introduction of such degradation into English life, although English indifference allowed it to persist and even took advantage of it.

Those of you who would read, in burning and often unpleasant words, the life of labour as seen by one of the workers should turn to *The Ragged-trousered Philanthropists*, by Robert Tressall, a house painter, who suffered, wrote his book, and died; or *Life in a Railway Factory*, by a Swindon hammerman now serving with the colours in India.[1]

Labour, or 'hands,' has been the one thing in the factory to be persistently cheated 'within the law.' Machinery cannot be cheated; it will clog, do less than its quota, get out of gear, break. In anticipation of its being 'scrapped' ample provision must be made in the balance sheet.

During the years of war wages have steadily risen in many parts of the area of labour, and in spite of rising prices very many workers are financially better off than hitherto. One of the unforeseen results of the long-drawn struggle has been a distinct tendency to eliminate extreme poverty. It may all come back, but the nation must put its mind, and the Church its inexhaustible spirit, into the work of reconstruction, and all will then be well. In the meantime, those who know the homes of working people are rejoiced at the increased health of mind and body which higher wages and regular employment have meant in many cases. The president of the

[1] Alfred Williams, 1877–1930.

Board of Education records with satisfaction the increased pressure on secondary school accommodation because more working people can afford to keep their children at school a few years longer.

But wages do not comprise the whole of the matter. A man may be well paid, but if the work he does is esteemed lightly, his spirit and life are depressed. We shall never know how much harm has been done by the contempt for labour on the part of those who could avoid sharing it. There is no satisfaction for us in the thought that those who expressed the contempt suffered the most, for, if 'one member suffer, all the members suffer with it.'

All work is honourable except unnecessary work. What shall we say of work which damages the community, or of dishonest or false work? Yet we tolerate work which poisons the community. There is far too much unworthy action in industry and in commerce. It forces men from the area of worship, especially those who are of an honest and true heart.

But some will think that, though labour is necessary and honourable, yet working men are too unpleasant, their habits too objectionable, their language too unrefined, for them to be welcomed, or even admitted, into the public life, much less the private life, of educated and refined people.

Let it be admitted that much work is dirty, that heavy labour induces forceful language, that coarse habits develop in rough surroundings; yet these are not the worst things in life, and they are remediable if only the community wills it.

The worst things in life are clever roguery, concealed immorality, euphemistic lies, and they are not the monopoly of any one class, and certainly not the characteristic of the working class who, on the whole, and I speak of those engaged in steady work, are generous, loyal, and true, and ready to take advantage of any opportunity for education or development which comes in their path. Their homes are often among the sweetest and purest, and they are ever ready to devote themselves to causes which they believe will benefit their fellows. The supreme need of our country is an increase in the number of these homes. To satisfy this we must have not only better housing conditions in town and country, an efficient system of education, and opportunities for pure entertainment, but a Church which is fearlessly determined to translate her principles into the common life. There can be no unhealthiness in any area of society without the whole area suffering. There can be no bad thing done in the recesses of a fetid slum which does not affect the purity of life in the homes of the rich.

The workers of England are members of the common body of humanity—they are potential members, in the fullness of the meaning of membership, of the Church, the body of Christ. Their welfare of body, mind, and spirit must be sought by church people in yearning love. If, with our imperfect knowledge, we hate them and their doings, as some at least seem to do at this time when the actions of working men and women, as heralded in newspapers, seem to militate against the true welfare of the nation, it is well for us to remember that there is a long history of the unwise treatment of labour by the community as a whole, and the false strike, the revolutionary action, may have had its beginnings in the disloyalty of church people to their own professed beliefs. The harbouring of hate—no matter what the inducement to do so—damages the real life of man. There must be constant endeavour to replace this destructive force by the unconquerable force of love.

There is a beautiful rendering of this thought of love set in a discourse of Father Zossima, a Christian figure in Dostoevsky's *Brothers Karamazov*:

If the wrongdoing of men fill thee with indignation and irresistible pain, so that thou desire even to take vengeance on the wrongdoers, then above all things resist that feeling. Go at once and seek suffering for thyself, as though thou thyself wert guilty of the wrongdoing. Accept that suffering, and endure it to the end, and so shall thine heart be comforted, and thou wilt understand how thyself art also guilty; for unto those evil-doers thou mightest have let shine thy light, even like the one sinless man; and thou didst not. If thy light had shone forth, it would have made clear the path for others, and the man who sinned would perchance have been saved by thy light. Or if it be that thou didst show thy light, and yet seest not that any are saved thereby; nevertheless stand thou firm, and doubt not the virtue of the heavenly light. Believe that if they have not been saved now, they will be saved hereafter; and if they should never be saved, then their sons will be saved; for thy light will not die even when thou art dead. The just man passeth away, but his light remaineth; and it is after the saviour's death that men are mostly saved. Mankind will reject and kill their prophets, but men love their martyrs and honour those whom they have done to death. Thou, moreover, art working for the whole, and for the future thou labourest. And look not for any outward reward, since, without that, thy reward on earth is already great; thine is the spiritual joy which only the righteous man findeth. . . . Love all men and all things; seek this rapture and ecstasy. Wet the earth with the tears of thy joy, and love those tears. Neither be ashamed of that ecstasy; cherish it highly, for it is the gift of God, a great gift; nor is it granted to many, but only to the elect.

Love all men. Love those who make, and build, and dig, for 'without these cannot a city be inhabited.' If their lives are not right, then the country cannot be right.

We have spoken of the damage caused by the contempt for labour, but the fear which rises out of distrust of labour is more destructive. If we are confident that labour will act rightly and, as a result, do not strive to obstruct its path, it will tend to do its perfect work. The days seem to be coming when the representatives of labour interests will take a large part in the government of England, if they do not actually control it. It is, of course, within our right to strive to put those people in power who will, we think, govern best. Indeed we should do our utmost to do so, but suspicion and fear of labour, as indeed of any other worthy section of the community, should be banished from our hearts if we would help our country and even secure a fair and equitable attitude towards the temporal interests of the Church.

It is now time to look at one or two positive principles.

I am convinced that God, working through society, does ordain men to specific work, for the carrying out of which He confers the necessary gifts and characteristics. The consequence of this is that man's highest blessedness consists in, or rather is, the direct result of his doing, simply, fearlessly, and uncomplainingly, the work for which his capacities and gifts fit him—no matter whether that work be ordinary manual labour or prophetic thinking. In order to help her members to act rightly in this direction the Church should strive with all her power to give to labour the consideration and honour which is inherently due to it.

The chief instrument lying to the hand of the nation for this purpose is the education system. The school, adapted to the needs of all, since it claims to concern itself with all, must seek, in a true spirit of humility before the wonder of child life, to discover capacity and, having discovered it, to see that it is developed, no matter what the financial cost. There is a present danger that, in view of fancied economic needs and the false gospel of organized force, the teaching in the schools will become overwhelmingly materialistic, whereas it must be dominated by a spiritual view of life, or fail to attain its true goal. The 'golden calf' claims a succession of worshippers, and has to be dethroned again and again in all ages.

This brief glance at the place of education in the national life must not blind us to the immense difficulty of developing a wise system. The process of education is long, and slow, and difficult to put into practice, but, if the schools will endeavour to satisfy the need for the right men to get to their right, or God-given, work, then from the outset the whole community will benefit, for, whatever mistakes are made, more men and women will have the opportunity to fulfil their beings than would otherwise have been the case without some such attempt having been made.

Every piece of right work done under right conditions is in harmony with worship—is indeed worship itself. It makes the members of the body thrill to Him who is Head.

I sometimes think that, in our human vision, the toiling masses of labour are outside the Church. It would indeed seem that only here and there do we find working men in any number who claim membership. The great bulk of them affect indifference, and a good proportion are hostile and contemptuous. And all this at a time when the true spirit of the working man, religious in its manifestations, expresses itself in many ways.

If you ask me: 'How are they to be brought back?' I can think of no other answer than: 'Simply as the direct result of those who are of the Church seeking to live the Christ life.' I do not think that by any device of intellect, or organization, men will be won. Understanding of the economic position and the social problem is good and essential, but such understanding in itself has no magnetic power, no saving health.

But in these days there are some who think and speak as though the masses could be won for Christ by a lowering of the standards of belief or practice, or by sanctimonious statements that the articles of our creed are capable of any interpretation which human wit may devise. I say the working man who thought that the Church was trying to come down to his fancied level would turn from it for ever. It would be far better to raise the standard, to be even more definite and clear in regard to fundamental dogma. Such steps would command his respect, compel his thought, and draw his spirit, if in all, around all, and through all there was the spirit of Christ manifesting itself in love to the uttermost of the poorest and most degraded of the people.

As we think of our blessed Lord, who loved the poor and called men of despised occupations to be His disciples, who sanctified human labour by sharing it, it is not hard to let our hearts go out to men unlike ourselves, but it will be very hard to alter our lives to harmonize with our new conceptions.

Still, there never was a time when it was more possible to make alterations than now. It is admittedly a time of reconstruction. Let us seize it 'by the forelock.' For changes will come, and will leave us little time in which to adapt ourselves, unless indeed we have foreseen them or taken the great precaution of exercising confidence in a spirit of love. Moreover, we may think of St. Paul who, brought up as he was 'at the feet of Gamaliel,' turned to tent-making. Few of us will be called upon to follow such an example, but we may yet have unexpected things to do. After all, it is not the work that matters so much as the spirit which we bring to it. When others suffer we suffer; when others are honoured we must rejoice. 'Ye are the body of Christ,' but far removed in strength and power from that body which shall be. To many it appears to be powerless on earth, swept out of its course by the temporal power of material things. But it is not so. The only power really at work is that of the Spirit.

Thank God it reveals itself daily in every act of mercy, generosity, and truth.

The day must come when the body of Christ on earth will be enriched by the whole nation—labourers, thinkers, prophets, and priests—and indeed by every nation. 'The nations of the earth do bring their glory and honour into it.'

'Ye are the body of Christ.' What a responsibility—an unbearable responsibility if the strength to meet it and the power to work came from elsewhere than from God. And such strength and such power work along the lines of the enduring truth: 'whether one member suffer, all the members suffer with it, or one member be honoured, all the members rejoice with it.'

8. IDEALS AS FACTS

(This article was a contribution to *The Way Out*, a volume of educational essays edited by Mr. Oliver Stanley and published by Humphrey Milford in May 1923. The volume appeared at a time when 'there was a revival of interest in both educational training and knowledge on the part of all kinds of people.' The article gives a detailed survey of the educational facilities for adults then existing in England, in every important sphere, rural, urban, and maritime.)

IF the ideal of an educated people is as reasonable as the foregoing chapters in this book would assume, then it becomes a matter of instant and paramount importance to discover how far and in what way it can be translated into present-day life. In any case the 'way out' is so supremely important to discover, that every bypath leading to it should be investigated throughout its length. That there is a revival of interest in both educational training and knowledge on the part of all kinds of people, quite exclusive of the needs of their daily life, is an established fact. A witness before the Adult Education Committee of the Board of Education, speaking of the desire of working girls for education in literature, history, and kindred subjects, used the words: 'It is almost an Elizabethan period.' But, if this be so, the average person who has not been concerned with the development of the various movements and institutes devoted to adult education which have risen, or are rising, in all part of England, will be perplexed as to how and in what way he shall take his part in the work which, it is to be assumed, he regards as essential.

At the outset it must be stated quite clearly and unmistakably that the best way for the majority of people to strengthen the work is by seeking education for themselves. This would seem to be a platitude but, as a matter of fact, if the majority of people who ask for facilities in education and training were prepared at the same time to seek them for themselves, then, obviously, the Adult Education movement would receive an accession of strength which it is impossible to estimate. Many will say: 'But we do this in our own ways—by maintaining an active interest in the proceedings of learned societies, by reading books, or by attendance at such lectures, concerts,

74

and dramatic representations as we approve, and which, in addition to affording us the recreation we desire after our day's work, both add to our knowledge and cultivate our taste'; but all this is not comparable in force to the expressed desire for, and willingness to attend, an organized course of lectures or a class, such as, for example, the Board of Education would be justified in supporting even in time of financial stringency. Of course, it would not be possible for every one to do this owing to the actual conflict of other duties, but every one who faces this problem must of necessity decide for himself or herself. The mere facing of it will set free new forces.

The principle we wish to establish, put in other words, is that the important thing in this connection is an increased demand on the part of all kinds of people for educational facilities, which may roughly be termed non-vocational, since they are concerned really with restoring balance to a man who has, of necessity, developed to a great extent one or other of his characteristics for the purposes of his livelihood or for the satisfaction of his reasonable desires. A concrete illustration will give point to this. In Czechoslovakia certain university professors discovered their need for adult education; that is, they found that they were engaged almost exclusively in intellectual work which made insufficient demand upon their physical powers, especially in relation to its application to creative work. They therefore turned in their leisure hours to the practice of ordinary manual processes such as are utilized in applied metal, leather, and woodwork. The suggestion that English university teachers should make a demand for their own further education invariably provokes a smile, but it is as reasonable for a craftsman to go to a university teacher and to say: 'It is essential for your good and for the good of the community that you should learn how to make a box,' as it is for the university professor to go to the craftsman and say: 'For the good of your soul it is necessary that you should study history, or literature, or poetry.' Experience has shown that the best organizers or directors of adult educational work are those who have at some time or another sought it for themselves. Many experiments in the past have proved abortive because people without such experience have sought to impose merely academic views and ideas upon those who they were pleased to think stood in need of education.

The appeal of the chapters of *The Way Out* is made to every possible type of man and woman within the community —those commonly termed educated, as well as those regarded as almost illiterate—who desire to make the best of themselves, and, more especially, to the men and women who are convinced that the increase in the numbers of those striving to reach that goal will tend to bring nearer that general and active participation in all the healthy aspects of the common life which a state of democracy makes possible. After all, let us be clear about it. Democracy is a state of society in which every individual not only has the opportunity to make the best of his, or her, own individual gifts, but actually takes advantage of the opportunity. Such a conception of society is, perhaps, idealistic, but if people to-day set their faces towards the achievement of it, however distant it may seem and be, instant results will accrue, and the ordinary life in the community of to-morrow will be on a higher level and set in a straighter course.

The whole educational activity of a people is in reality directed and moulded by the proportion of adults who have gained a deep and spiritual perception of what education really is, simply because as a result of valuing it they have searched for it and not contented themselves merely with acquiescing in such an extension of it in the community as would make no serious addition to the rates and taxes.

Thus, the argument that the development of adult education can be left to look after itself because of the more pressing needs of children and adolescents is disposed of by anticipation. There is no possible way by which an effective educational system can be created other than by increasing genuine belief in education among adults. The gibe of Mr. Bernard Shaw, that the school is the parents' defence against the child, is not wholly unmerited, as it would be if parents welcomed opportunities of study for themselves.

The problem of adult education may roughly be divided into rural and urban. At first sight it will seem that the town dweller would be most responsive to the appeal. As a matter of fact there is no evidence to support this. Almost every experiment which has been carried out on right lines in English villages in recent years has proved successful. It has been almost astonishingly easy to get a large proportion of village men and women to study such subjects as history and literature when the delights of doing so have been revealed to them in a way devoid of pedantry or of obvious desire to 'do them good.' Moreover, there are many like the village women who shuddered at the idea of school and history, but were eager to hear about 'life in the old times.' The chief difficulty about village work is not to obtain students, but to meet, without undue strain, the expenses of teachers or lecturers who have to come from a distance. A further difficulty is inherent in the fact that in spiritual and mental work of this kind so much depends on personality that successful work in a village may decline and even vanish when a person who has organized, or inspired, it leaves the neighbourhood. The effect of the war upon educational work in many villages proved to be disastrous in this respect, as indeed does the emigration of the most adventurous young farm-workers.

In the tranquil days of 1910 to 1914 the bodies which did most were the Workers' Educational Association and the Adult School movement, particularly the former. For a long time the only adult educational activity in many villages was the more or less effective mothers' meeting. The men had nothing but the inn, the chapel, or the church. Of the three, the first proved easily the most attractive, and, in spite of the destructive nature of its stock-in-trade, it did provide facilities for discussion and exchange of ideas. The benefits arising directly out of bell-ringing or singing in the choir, as well as local preaching, have been inestimable. To-day village clubs and men's and women's institutes [1] have arisen in a very large

---

[1] Over two thousand women's institutes are federated in the National Federation of Women's Institutes; five hundred and twenty village clubs are affiliated to the Village Clubs Association.

number of villages, whilst the Y.M.C.A. and such bodies as
the English Folk Dance Society are continually increasing
their activities. The dweller in rural England who would
assist in this kind of work need have no difficulty in coming
into contact with the organizations in his own village or with
a number of bodies anxious to take every opportunity to
develop new fields of work. Every possible kind of genuine
gift or capacity for service can be utilized.

The term 'Rural Community Council' has been suggested
largely by the efforts in the United States, but the method
adopted is singularly applicable to organizing work in English
villages. In Oxfordshire a Rural Community Committee
has been at work for three years. It unites for common
purposes the Red Triangle Federation, the Village Clubs
Association, the Workers' Educational Association, and the
Oxford University Tutorial Classes Committee, as well as
the county officials dealing with education and agriculture.
It set to work to develop a rural library scheme, and six
months after its initiation forty-seven villages were being
supplied regularly with books. This work having been
accomplished, the attention of the council was devoted to
the development of music and drama.

In individual villages social councils have been formed
representing the organizations and interests existing in the
village. To take a typical case: 'In Sparsholt and Lainston,
comprising a population of some three hundred, a Village
Social Council has been formed, upon which are represented
the Parish Council, the Allotment Holders, the Cricket and
Football Clubs, the School, the Flower Show Association, the
Friendly Societies, the Farmers' and Labourers' Unions, the
Landowners, the Library, the Mothers' Union, the Nursing
Association, the religious bodies, the Men's Club and Institute, and the Women's Institute.'[1] Certainly there are
now no lack of organizations in many small villages in England.
The problem of the adult educationist is to see that they do
actually make for increased strength in body and mind. A

---

[1] *Memorandum on Rural Development* (National Council of Social Service,
33 Bloomsbury Square, London, W.C.).

village council operating rightly can contribute at once to this important end. It seems probable that there will be a rapid development in county organizations, inasmuch as the Carnegie United Kingdom Trustees (acting at the request of a committee of the National Council of Social Service, of which the Speaker of the House of Commons is the president, and Professor W. G. S. Adams the chairman) have agreed to supply funds for a central committee and may, under certain conditions, assist a limited number of counties by way of experiment. If this experiment proves successful then there is no doubt that increased funds will be forthcoming, and, later, reasonable demands can be made upon the Treasury at a time when, as may be hoped, British finance will not be so hampered by the need for economy.

The whole question of village work is entrancing in all its aspects. It gives immediate results. There is no need to stress the advantages accruing; they are obvious. One word of warning must be uttered, however. The cinema, owing at least in part to the lethargy of religious and educational bodies, is very poorly expressed in English villages. The films exhibited in the ordinary village picture-house are, as a rule, both poor and sensational. Perhaps it is not yet too late, and some method of exhibiting really good and approved motion-pictures may yet be devised. There are now many film interpretations of classic novels which would do nothing but good if shown in any suitable village hall or room. Beyond all this there should be vans, containing books, gramophones, and cinematograph, travelling to the remotest and poorest hamlets, earning what money is possible, but subsidized to the extent of a reasonable deficit. In any case it is not yet too late for controlling the community use of broadcasting by wireless. Apart from the film and wireless those who would help village life should see to it that the rural community gets good music and good lectures. Musicians like Sir Walford Davies prefer the gramophone records of standard music to the cheap and nasty compositions which so often are the only basis for the development of musical taste. A community-controlled and not too accessible gramophone should be possessed by every village. The idea that country folk do not appreciate good music is absurd. Experiments made in Oxfordshire before the war in taking classical music to village audiences were entirely successful. Since the war, experiments promoted by County Education Committees and by the Carnegie United Kingdom Trust have demonstrated the same truth. Ordinary village people know the best when they hear it.

In any consideration of purely educational facilities, whether rural or urban, the question inevitably arises whether every member of the community should be expected, or ought, to use them. The doctrine of universal desire for education cannot be too emphatically stated, but the desire will only express itself in harmony with the gifts and momentum of the individual. In other words, there are diversities of gifts and interests, and it is idle to attempt to force interest where there is none. It is absurd, for example, to suggest that all village people are capable of gaining benefit from attendance at classes; there is only a certain proportion who, spending their time in doing so, are spending it the best way. There is, in point of fact, too great a disposition on the part of the educationist to regard as useless for any other purpose those who will not utilize the facilities he sets up. That is foolish and absurd. There are village labourers who may conceivably be spending their time better in manual activity about their houses and gardens than in attending any of the corporate educational efforts of the village. Scholarship is necessary, but only in those people fit to be scholars. Yet, when all is said and done, there are few normal persons in any village who would find their true development apart from corporate effort. The best education for any man or woman is that which develops the maximum strength of body and mind. The most that can be demanded of any individual is that he should consider in all seriousness, and with proper guidance, the best way of utilizing his time apart from unnecessary selfish interests. In any case the educationist, in considering an entire population, must not regard his classes as a species of philosophers' stone for all and sundry; neither does he win any success—rather the reverse—if he induces people to attend specific classes when they would otherwise be better employed.

Before turning to the urban problem it may be well to look at one of the most recent educational experiments which is neither urban nor rural, but is concerned with workers on ships. Just as in the case of villages, reasonably conducted experiments have produced uniform results which are full of encouragement. Yet, when the work was projected, ship-owners and others regarded it as fantastic and incapable of being brought into operation. Nevertheless encouragement was received from educationists among shipowners, and the work was initiated by financial assistance from the Chamber of Shipping, the leading trade unions, and the Carnegie United Kingdom Trust. In a very short time it was demon-strated that ordinary seafarers, whether on long or short voyages, would read the best books in the English language. After a few voyages the proportion of such readers in a ship's company has been known to rise to seventy-five per cent. Little has been done yet. Only fifty ships are in commission, but, after all, each ship is an institution and a moving one at that. There are eight thousand ships in the British Mercan-tile Marine, and three thousand of them at least should carry libraries, whilst the workers on the other five thousand should be in contact with a book service. Other experiments are being carried out with both cinematograph and gramophone, the latter with the assistance of Sir Walford Davies. The whole of this experiment proves once again the universality of demand, and it affords opportunity for the active co-opera-tion of those who are interested in seafarers.[1]

A host of institutions now jostle one another in the towns. The whole of the nineteenth century is full of the records of experiments of one sort or another made by working men's colleges, co-operative societies, mechanics' institutes, adult schools, and trade unions. The research work of Mr. A. E. Dobbs, published so far up to 1850,[2] is full of encouraging

[1] The Seafarers' Education Service had been founded in 1920.
[2] A. E. Dobbs, *Education and Social Movements, 1700–1850* (1919), Longmans.
* D

detail. Since 1850 the Working Men's Colleges, the University Extension movement, and the Workers' Educational Association have all been started, and the Adult School movement revived and stimulated. The Mechanics' Institute movement has, however, failed to increase in strength. In every town one or other of these organizations is at work, and sometimes all of them. They can be approached either locally or through their central offices.

At the end of the nineteenth century the chief desire was for the improved education of working men and women, who have demonstrated in the twentieth century that they are quite ready to undertake this work. The whisper is now beginning to be heard that one of the chief problems of to-day is not merely the education of the working man and woman, but of the middle and upper classes. Be that as it may, it is quite clear that working men and women will reach out to develop their own education in co-operation with scholars and educational administrators, and it may be well for other than the workers to seek in their own way to secure their own development. Yet education of this sort must never be organized on a class basis. It is better that all sections of the community should co-operate, but, even so, the ultimate result may be best brought about by adults pursuing their education according to their own inclinations and in the surroundings which they like and which are familiar to them.

Among the characteristic institutions which should be in every town are the University Extension lectures provided by Oxford and Cambridge, or the local university. These should bring to the town the best and latest thoughts conveyed in a popular way to people who are unable to attend classes. This work should remain in the hands of the universities, and not fall entirely into those of the lecturers themselves or of their agencies.

Direct instances of the effect of a succession of University Extension courses may be discovered and examined in many small towns. In large centres, such as Sheffield, Nottingham, Reading, and Exeter, they have proved to be the inspirational, if not the actual, nucleus of university colleges.

At Hebden Bridge, in Yorkshire, where the courses were substantially supported and made possible by members of the local co-operative enterprises, a real educational tradition has been established. The actual lectures have ceased, but the Hebden Bridge Literary and Scientific Society has been in active work for seventeen years. It possesses a library of a thousand volumes, and is organized in mathematical, historical, literary, astronomical, physical science, and photographic sections. The whole of the literary and scientific lore of a most interesting district is explored and presented for the profit and enjoyment not only of its three hundred members, but of all and sundry. There are sixty definite educational fixtures in the current syllabus of the society.

The remarkable development of University Extension work in Northumberland and Durham in the period between 1879 and 1887 has influenced the mind of a whole countryside. Even though the system was broken, yet it left its disciples everywhere, and their presence is proved by the educational work of village clubs and co-operative societies as well as by the frequent existence in the poorest homes of well-selected books.

In addition to University Extension lectures there should also be special classes consisting of twelve or twenty-four lectures of a less popular nature, at which the members should be encouraged to make every attendance, to take an active part in the discussions following the lectures, and to write at least one essay. Although to-day many bodies organize classes such as these, the bulk of this work has hitherto been carried out by the Workers' Educational Association. Prior to 1903 there had been a considerable amount of isolated educational effort. The association, founded in that year, was in essence and in fact a new creation. It aimed not merely at uniting the universities, trade unions, and co-operative societies together for educational purposes, but it endeavoured to fuse into one all the forces which might be expected to contribute to the education of working men and women. It was essentially democratic in character, and made its permanent contribution to the cause of educational progress by bringing, not merely into the area of its influence, but into its actual organization, universities and working-class bodies and scholars. The growth of the association was rapid. It was a national body, devoted entirely to education, and through the enthusiasm and devotion of the members of its local branches in different parts of the country, its position rapidly became established.

Parallel with these courses there should be the University Tutorial Classes, which members can only join if they pledge themselves to make every possible attendance for three years, and to write regular essays. The standard reached in many cases equals that of a university honours degree in the particular subject of study, and none but the best tutors are selected for such work. The classes are under the auspices of joint committees, which exist in connection with practically all the universities and university colleges. These committees are composed of an equal number of representatives from the university and from working-class movements, the latter being nominated by the Workers' Educational Association. These classes represent for the vast majority of the students the crown of the adult educational system, and they constitute in a very special way the peculiar contribution of this country to adult educational method throughout the world.

These three types of effort, therefore, University Extension lectures, One-Year Classes, and University Tutorial Classes, should give in humanistic subjects everything needed in the way of direct educational inspiration, for out of them, or around them, spring many types of effort and every kind of existing activity will be illumined and strengthened.

The Act of 1918 marks an epoch in the history of adult education. It is there made plain that local education authorities are to include the education of adults in their schemes, and whilst this may for the moment not be positively enforced, yet the whole attitude of local education authorities has been transformed. They differ in their approach; some prefer to utilize and assist voluntary bodies, whilst others attempt to render them unnecessary so far as formal teaching, apart from stimulation and recreation, is concerned. The whole matter is, however, receiving for the first time patient and careful consideration. It is unlikely that organization will be systematized. Probably both the methods of direct and indirect provision of adequate facilities will be adopted in the same areas, and some form of co-operation between adjacent and similar statutory areas will be developed.

In the early days of the Workers' Educational Association, a body which has not attempted so far to secure premises for its educational work, but has relied almost entirely upon the hospitality of others, it was frequently said that its activities would inevitably inspire the creation of working men's colleges or settlements. This was probably due to the fact that the Working Men's College, founded by Frederick Denison Maurice in 1853, had the same intention and was constructed on the same principles, if not by the same methods, as the Workers' Educational Association. Moreover there is no finer expression of human fellowship than the college life of England; at the Working Men's College it is known as the 'college spirit.'

But apart from the McKnight Memorial College at Chorley and Holybrook House, Reading, little has been done in this direction by the Workers' Educational Association. It has been too busy organizing its widespread system of classes. It was left to Mr. Horace Fleming to demonstrate the power of a local educational settlement or community centre. At Beechcroft in Birkenhead he has provided a home for the many movements which are at work in the vicinity, and built up a real structure of adult education. Movements which are opposed to one another outside the walls of the settlement find unity as they participate in the activities within.

It is in the creation of further 'Beechcrofts' that much of the hope for the future lies. An Educational Settlements Association has been constructed, and at places like York and Letchworth much forward work has been accomplished. The older residential settlements, of which Toynbee Hall was the pioneer, have many other duties to fulfil, but Cambridge House, in south London, and Mansfield House, in east London, are typical of the effort to meet the educational needs of adult workers.

Quite apart from the directly educational associations and institutions, yet working more or less with them, stand the movements such as the co-operative, the trade union, and the adult school which have been constructed for definite purposes. These are now showing an increased tendency to develop educational institutions of their own. The co-operative movement has a long educational record, but the needs of trade unionists so far as residential facilities are concerned have been met, as far as possible, by Ruskin College and the Central Labour College, which is definitely partisan in the Marxian sense, while thousands of trade unionists have been through Workers' Educational Association classes. Recently a new committee known as the Workers' Educational Trade Union Committee has been formed, which will in general endeavour to exercise control in regard to the education of trade unionists, whilst utilizing all the opportunities which it approves, whether provided by voluntary or statutory bodies. As for the Adult School movement, it is adding increasingly to its traditional study of the life and teaching of Jesus all forms of secular adult education, and has many guest houses and centres under its auspices.

The tendency of movements to meet the needs of their own members is natural and healthy. It is only in the full force of the inspiration of their own immediate and chosen fellows that men and women will be able to do their best work. Moreover, there is the constant and laudable desire to enrich the movement which has meant so much to them. Many, for example, have found in the co-operative movement a kind of secular religion which has illumined their lives. The influence of this counts for much.

If, however, colleges, such as that suggested in the scheme of the co-operative movement, are created, then they must be included in a large and comprehensive synthesis of adult educational effort which includes the universities. In labour circles it is not uncommon to hear adumbrated as an ideal the labour university, but the more far-sighted labour leaders see that a university—or the supreme educational institution of any people—must be open to all sincere students and teachers of good will. The influence of the universities of Oxford and Cambridge increased enormously as soon as the Test Acts were removed and they ceased to be close institutions of the Church of England.

There is a growing habit of attending summer and vacation schools on the part of serious-minded men and women. As a general rule for the educational progress of adults it is best that they should attend local classes and utilize the summer schools rather than that they should make a break in their occupation and their lives by going into residence at university or other colleges. Only those ought thus completely to change the circumstances of their lives who are really and indubitably scholars. For the rest residence at working people's colleges or at the ordinary colleges of a university is too expensive a matter in comparison with attendance at local classes or summer schools. Yet the existing experiments, which have been constructed at much sacrifice and cost, such as Ruskin College at Oxford, Fircroft at Birmingham, and the Working Women's College at Beckenham, should be maintained and strengthened.

There is a strong and indubitable case to be made out for the working man and woman leaving working-class life and going into one or other of the colleges when they can serve the community either by increasing its democratic spirit, or adding to its scholarship. But it would be a doubtful and dangerous expedient to construct at great cost little colleges which would always be in danger of breeding sectionalism. This is quite apart from the argument that movements might find it well to establish colleges of their own, but these must be in their own scheme, and designed to develop and concentrate their forces in order that they may the better help their national system.

There is no need to enumerate all the opportunities for active work or for the expression of practical sympathy which face the man or woman who has arrived at a state of conviction as to the necessity of finding a way out in our time from the confusing mass of problems which confront the entire community. Suffice it to say, that not yet has the time of real and forceful development arrived. A new synthesis is necessary, based on the results of recent experiments. Such a synthesis will inevitably require patient investigation and research, carried out through the pooling of experience gained by workers in all these different movements. To this end the Board of Education has recently set up an advisory committee which has published reports dealing with various phases of the problem, while for the majority of the active workers in the different organizations the British Institute of Adult Education[1] provides a common meeting-ground. At the same time, through its representative membership this latter body is enabled to urge upon the community the vital importance of adult education and to concern itself generally with the removal of these difficulties which affect the movement as a whole.

Perhaps suggestions towards the solution of some of the problems involved may be obtained from other countries. The bulletins of the World Association for Adult Education[2] convince us that there is widespread development throughout the civilized world, and the information bureau of the Association proves that England is in many respects behind other countries, although it alone has united its universities and the organizations of the workers. If only it can help other countries to do likewise, by the suggestion of its example, a great contribution will have been made towards international development. Universities have always co-operated with one another because science and letters know no national boundaries. The workers are beginning to co-operate along lines of industrial development and mutual interest. If to this can be added the joint working of all of them for educational development, then each alike will benefit, and not only they, but the whole of our common humanity. The reconstruction of society in the world depends upon the co-operation of the different interests in pursuing a line of action which leads to noble and pure ends. Of all possible ends the education of the people stands out as most clearly necessary.

It cannot be achieved as a mere intellectual process; it is

[1] Founded in 1921.　　　　[2] Founded in 1918.

also both physical and spiritual, and its eager response is to the motions of wisdom which is at once the life and inspiration of the world. Knowledge is not education; it is but the fuel burnt in a flame which comes from the heart of the world and which makes all things new. Burnt in any other way it smoulders and suffocates. Of all the gifts showered on man knowledge is the most dangerous. The educated man uses it aright and fulfils the purpose of his desire. No one can avoid knowledge altogether; it is the condition of life in the world. But after a certain necessary minimum few people need identically the same knowledge. There is a diversity of gifts.

So the ideal of adult education is the fulfilment of capacity, the expression of the life of every man and woman at its best. All around are manifold opportunities which, if seized, will develop and help to bring about gradual progress, through correspondence with the eternal laws which makes life at once purer, wiser, and more beautiful.

9. EXCEPT YE BECOME AS LITTLE CHILDREN

(The fifth annual conference of the British Institute of Adult Education was held at Cambridge in 1926. The following sermon was delivered in the chapel of Trinity College, and later published in the *Journal of Adult Education*. The address has for its main theme the need for the spirit of the child in adult education.)

AS a basis for what I propose to say I will read some sayings of Jesus as collected and arranged from the gospels by Dr. Mackail, a fellow worker in the cause of adult education:

Suffer little children to come to me and forbid them not, for of such is the kingdom of heaven.

Take heed how ye despise one of these little ones, for, I tell you, in heaven their angels always behold the face of my Father who is in heaven. Even so it is not the will of your Father in heaven that one of these little ones should perish. Whoever, therefore, shall humble himself as this little child, is greatest in the kingdom of heaven, and whosoever shall receive one such little child in my name receives me, and whoever receives me, receives not me but him who sent me.

What was it that you disputed among yourselves by the way? I tell you of a truth whoever shall not receive the Kingdom of God as a little child shall not enter into it.

Yes, I tell you, except ye are converted and become as little children, you shall not enter into the kingdom of heaven.

I thank thee, O Father, Lord of heaven and earth, because thou hast hid these things from the wise and prudent and hast revealed them to babes. Even so, Father, for so it seemed good in thy sight.

A clear message delivered by Jesus in these sayings is that true and lasting work is done by those who, whilst expressing the spirit of little children, have not allowed the fires of the life eternal to be damped down by that material of the world, which either because it is out of place, or because there is too much of it, cannot be consumed for the comfort and light of men.

As for true and lasting work, it is of that Kingdom into which no one shall enter, unless he does so in the right and might of a little child.

The Kingdom of Heaven is surely, in one of its aspects, the

area occupied here and now by all those acts and thoughts which are true: that is which are in harmony with, which do not antagonize, the perfect working of natural and spiritual law, and which consequently tend to make men what they are intended to be, magnificent, splendid workers in the creative evolution of the world.

The rhythm of life in these sayings runs from the Father— through Jesus—to a little child, and only as a child can man harmonize with it.

If there is anything characteristic of the life and teaching of Jesus, it is surely that the little, the simple and the pure, are the great dominating forces and facts.

> I come in the little things,
> Saith the Lord.
> My starry wings
> I do forsake,
> Love's highway of humility to take:
> Meekly I fit My stature to your need.
> In beggar's part
> About your gates I shall not cease to plead—
> As man, to speak with man—
> Till by such art
> I shall achieve My Immemorial Plan,
> Pass the low lintel of the human heart.[1]

It is a hard lesson for men who are clever and skilled, who know so much, to learn that their real power is derived from the attributes of childhood, that the eyes of babes see the eternal verities.

Yet there is inspiration in the thought that the nearer a man can get to the things that are common to all men, the nearer he will get to the Kingdom of Heaven.

It is a gospel of comfort to the simple—that they have in them here on earth all the essentials of the citizenship of heaven. Men cannot go back on their steps; but they can strive with all their power to get their knowledge and skill into right relationship with their abiding spirits which shone most clearly in the days of their childhood, just because they were not then so heavily overlaid with the materials and facts of society and the temporal world.

[1] Evelyn Underhill, *Divine Immanence.*

They can do this the more easily because the advance of knowledge in these later days has demonstrated the inherent power of pure and simple forces, both in human and in natural life, even as it has provided support for the affirmations of simple faith, the things hidden from 'the wise and prudent but revealed unto babes.'

A wider diffusion of tried and tested knowledge than existed in the nineteenth century has given rise to a new spirit of understanding. The thoughts of patient and humble seekers after truth are not so often misconstrued by the ignorant prejudiced. 'Toleration of opinion,' said Sir William Bragg, in a recent Boyle lecture, 'is a recognized virtue. The curiosity of the present position is that opposite opinions have to be held or used by the same individual in the faith that some day the combined truth may be made plain.' As a direct result of this recognition of the limitations of human knowledge, unity where it is not apparent is regarded as implicit in all real work. Moreover, men are not now expected to possess active perception of all true things equally; there are diversities of gifts.

The scientist is true to his quest if he refuses to utter a word that his reason, probing and selecting the facts, does not justify, but untrue if he, overstepping his limits, seeks to bind the legitimate thoughts and conclusions, even when they seem to contradict his own, of faithful workers in other fields utilizing other means.

His work is clear. His tasks are different from those of the musician or the poet who, borne on the wings of inspiration, feel that divine afflatus which surely is heaven bound. ''Tis we musicians know.'

There are, of course, men who have got hold of a piece of knowledge, and at once set out to dogmatize on the how and wherefore of man's action. They are so blinded by their achievements that they cannot see that every attempt made by any one person or school to dominate life has led to artificial work, to destruction and decay. They are sometimes called the 'intellectuals'—they are so clever. They are clever. But, thank God, a democracy will never give itself away to the teaching and the dictates of any one who is 'clever'; a democracy will put him in his place, and because he has discovered one thing it will not allow him to subject, or try to subject, the rest of human life to his little piece.

But our intellectuals who tell us what to do and what is going to happen are not so much to be blamed as the people who round about them are not doing their work properly—their own work. The average man has a work. Each genuine worker in the world has some contribution to make to the whole—his contribution, not an imitation of someone else's. Health and sanity in human life and opinion depend directly upon the proportion of quite ordinary people who are using their powers to the utmost in childlike faith.

After all, what is man? Just a perplexed child in the flowing tide of the stream of life. What is life? Where does it come from?

Scientists are careful in these days, very careful. They know that there are mysteries in simple phenomena deeper than their research has ever probed or their imagination plumbed. 'Life is regarded,' says Dr. Russell, 'as a continuous process manifested by individuals who strive actively, albeit blindly, to achieve in spite of circumstances the end and aim of their being.'[1]

What even is matter? 'The limit of our knowledge is that at present matter exists,' says Dr. Jeans, 'or at least has enough of the attributes of existence to make us think it exists. As to what, if anything, it was before it was matter we know nothing.'[2]

Leaving the incomprehensible, though familiar matter and life, let us turn to the comprehensible and think of man in the midst of the vastness and the minuteness of things—things that can be perceived, and measured, even though they defy and bewilder our imagination.

Spiral nebulae have been detected at a distance of 1,000,000 light years; 'something like 250,000 times as far as the nearest of the stars, which are about 250,000 times the distance of the

---

[1] *Proceedings, Aristotelian Society*, 1922–3.
[2] *Evolution in the Light of Modern Knowledge—Cosmogony* (Blackie & Sons).

sun, which in turn is 250,000 times as far from us as Edinburgh is from London. Of course, we cannot see the nebulae as they now are, but only as they were a million years ago.' [1]

Let us turn from the heights above and around to the infinite depths on a grain of sand; composed of countless atoms, each, it is affirmed, a solar system, electrons revolving as planets round the nucleus, a central sun. An imaginative scientist only this past week—I do not know how to value his authority exactly—has asserted the possibility of life on the electron. Absurd. And yet the atom in relation to the earth is something like the solar system in relation to the universe. As for such minute life, every bacteriologist knows that there are infinite forms which no eye has ever seen and no instrument—using ultra-violet or any other rays—has ever revealed. Some of them, progenitors of disease, have been discovered in fluids only by their effects on organisms. In such a field adult education claims its heroes; Gye—increasingly recognized as the discoverer of fundamental facts in the causation of cancer and the creator of a new medical technique—was inspired by it, as was Barnard his colleague —hatter in working hours and microscopist out of them— the persistent and progressive revealer of the invisible.

Merely to think of these things induces the certitude that man in his most experienced and accomplished power has no claim for consideration to be other than as a little child. It was the immortal Newton, son of this college, who asserted that in the search for truth he was even as a child gathering pebbles on a vast seashore.

Truly man on the lowest level can do no other than seek to express in the terms of his body and mind the stream of life force. Such seeking will be directed and illumined if he is wise enough to realize the immanence of God in human life, and become a glorious and happy quest if he practises the perception of the abiding companionship of the Holy Spirit. To further such realizations and speed such a quest this chapel was constructed and dedicated.

As for man, be he wise or unwise, he is the creature of

---

[1] Jeans's *Cosmogony*.

heredity, the product of a long past. He seems, as it were, to have gathered into his being all the attributes and powers of innumerable generations of forbears; and these reveal themselves in the little child. He has instincts, he has intuitions, and they seem to be quite independent of anything he may acquire. He seems to share these with the animals. But then he has intellect. He can acquire knowledge. He can make tools. He can use them. Therein lies his difference from the animals. Even so, the right relationship of knowledge, his tools and the things he makes, to the reality of his life is an age-old problem.

I was reminded as I came along the streets to this conference of an objection which was made at our conference last year to the attempt to draw students into London continuation classes by the picture of a determined workman hewing steps in a gigantic pyramid, in order that he might climb it successfully. Whether the objection was valid or not, we need not pause to determine. The pyramid has vanished from the hoardings, and has been replaced by a lamp revealing the light of knowledge. 'The spirit of man is the candle of the Lord.' Perchance knowledge is the fuel which the spirit must burn in order that the expression of the man shall be complete in the terms of his body and mind. The true man sheds light in dark places. Light is the supreme symbol as it is the ultimate purpose of his life. It is at once the inspiration and desire of the university. 'The Lord my light' has been blazoned on the arms of Oxford for nearly eight centuries. 'Let there be light' is the prayer of the half-century-old university of California.

So it is clear that knowledge must be used by men, for the diffusion of light, who, in the power of the eternal spirit, have become as little children.

Let us pause to think briefly of some of the characteristics of child life at its best. There is no one except the hardened cynic who does not receive a fresh measure of inspiration as he looks into the clear, unclouded eyes of a little child. What, then, is the purpose of education but to ensure that men and women shall continue to be as pure as children whilst they exercise the activities and powers which God has given them?

A characteristic of the child is that it can wonder. It finds reason for wonder everywhere. Happy are we if we can remember the days when every little, new thing was a concern of delight. Happy are we, thrice happy, if we can feel that wonder now. The child has no consciousness of its importance. It has confidence and faith in those about it just as we have confidence and faith in the workings, shall we say? of natural law, confidence that it will go on with the same persistence, unaltering. Then it is not concerned with others. It leaves others alone; it does not want to interfere. It wants to enjoy, to express itself, to expand itself, and to do things because of the sheer delight that self-expression brings. It finds happiness in the use of its own small limbs, in the exercise of itself. To be is enough. To be, and not to succeed. Surely in these things—in wonder, lack of self-consciousness, confidence, and faith, the leaving of others alone, in doing things for their own sake, and in the actual joy of existence, in these things we can find the dynamic, the *élan vital* of adult education.

In the days immediately prior to the new movement in adult education which promises so much, young men and women would come and say: 'We want to teach.' Now those of them who really understand say: 'We want to learn.' In so far as they have adopted this attitude, they have become as little children. The secret of adult education in one of its aspects is surely that he who teaches must become in spirit, and therefore in fact, like unto those who are students. Grown men and women hate to be merely taught. They respond to the idea of studying with one who, really equipped with knowledge, is willing to help, whilst respecting their own experience and knowledge. Every teacher knows that no one can help little children so much as those who can become like unto them, one with their spirit. As it is with children, so it is with adults.

The early Tutorial Class always seemed to me, in its sheer delight, like a gathering of children, so full it was of happiness and faith. I shall never forget the rapture of those early days —the joy of them—and the rapture persists and expands in the widespread movement of to-day.   There was no 'breaking up' until time was far spent, or buildings had to be closed; two, three, four hours they would go on.   Yes, in the real pursuit of learning, tutors and students are alike children.

In the High School movement of Denmark, perhaps the most wonderful of all the adult educational movements of the century, there is evident the same childlike spirit, the same joyousness in the simple and the pure.   Grundtvig, its prophet, and Kold, who interpreted him, were children indeed, and never more so than in the days of their mature and learned power.

Only a week ago we were in the Folk University at Rotterdam.   One who understands and works for it said: 'People in this town don't like sometimes the Folk University.   But they don't understand.   We like it because every one is so happy, just happy.'   There are ten thousand men and women who enjoy, in one way or another, that Folk University.   We saw them in their classes, and we saw them at their play.   We saw them present a scene from one of the sacred plays of a great Dutch poet.   It seemed that they were just happy children playing in a park.

Let us think, too, of the cloud of witnesses everywhere about us, and especially in this college.   I will not interfere with our thought this morning by bringing forward records of work spoiled by those who have not the spirit of children.

John Brown Paton, an underlying and positive force in all modern English movement for adult education, died at the age of eighty-three.   I saw him on his death-bed, and it seemed to me that he was even then facing life as a little child, conscious not of himself but of the unending work.   Throughout his long life he was, even whilst stern in his judgment of wrong, as confident and unafraid as a child—indeed, he was ever conscious of the abiding presence of his heavenly Father.

Always it has seemed to me that the men and women who have, without complexity, done the real and lasting work for adult education, untroubled by assertive intellect, have been just simple children playing and working in the power of that wisdom which, coming from the heavens of God, 'goes through all things by reason of its pureness.'

Then, too, I recall the early days of the Workers' Educational Association in this college. Working men came expecting university dons to be forbidding and unapproachable gigantic creations, and found them like little children, ready to play, ready to sing songs.

I must pay tribute to one who did so much to inspire us, and who was indeed a little child—Arthur Charlwood Turner, known to some of us here. He gave his life in simple faith even as so many of his fellows, working men and scholars, in that long-drawn war which smote the world as a foul happening because so many denied the purifying truth of the child spirit.

I would fain remember others, members of this college, who went out in the main as children and whose names appear on that sad long list in this chapel:

> Salute the sacred dead,
> Who went and who return not. Say not so . . .
> We rather seem the dead, that stayed behind.
> Blow, trumpets, all your exultation blow,
> But never shall their aureoled presence lack . . .
>   They come transfigured back,
> Secure from change in their high-hearted ways,
> Beautiful evermore, and with the rays
> Of morn on their white shields of Expectation.[1]

And in duty bound I would pay tribute to the memory of Harry Percival Smith, a member of this college, 1874–7, who revealed to me the power of the child spirit in the days of my young manhood, when I was apt to forget it. He was father of one of our workers in the office of this British Institute —he died two days ago; and in his own college I hold it a duty and a privilege to remember him.

Then just one last thought. The development of the child spirit in adult education will help, both directly and indirectly, the little ones actually at school. If I had time I could show how much of the attitude towards children in schools resulting in wiser educational methods and more generous provision of facilities has been induced by childlike people engaged in adult education, whether as working men and women or as university scholars.

[1] James Russell Lowell.

Christ the great Teacher taught, and every true teacher since the world began has taught, that the child spirit is the spirit which enables men to do and conquer.

So we go on to the full splendour of our lives—not by forcing ourselves back into the ways of children but by allowing the child spirit to rise through our hearts and minds. We ask our way, our faces thitherwards, to the City of God, which will surely be reached in so far as all men strive to make the best of themselves. For adult education is in the broadest sense for all, and especially for the simple and unafraid, not merely for those few who seem to be clever, who wish to succeed, who desire qualification and have the will to power. As men everywhere realize this, and come forward to take their unobtrusive yet necessary part, so shall we 'build Jerusalem in England's green and pleasant land.'

I love to think of us all, in the child spirit, moving on to the splendour intended for us, living and working and studying as those

> Amid this loud stunning tide of human care and crime
> With whom the melodies abide of the everlasting chime,
> Who carry music in their heart
> Through dusty street and wrangling mart,
> Plying their daily task with busier feet,
> Because their secret souls a holy strain repeat.[1]

A procession of men and women with faces like those of little children going happily with them, happy with the inherent happiness of true human life as planned by the Father, revealed by the Son, and made possible in the power of the Holy Spirit.

May God Himself help us to bring it about by enabling us to reassert the spirit of our own childhood, which is the expression on earth of His spirit—Father He surely is: except we become as little children we shall not, cannot, enter into the Kingdom of Heaven, and all our work in the field of adult education will be profitless and vain, even though we, and others, may foolishly admire it.

[1] John Keble, *The Christian Year* (St. Matthew's Day).

10. THE CITIZENSHIP OF THE TEACHER

(This foundation oration was delivered at the London Day Training College—now the Institute of Education, University of London—on 7th March 1927, before a body of teachers and students in training. The ideals and duties of the perfect teacher are discussed. In order that the full life of man may be lived, the individual called upon to teach needs a plan of action, and should realize that the school is 'an institution in the city of all men.' The mind of man is made creative through the power of the Spirit.)

ALL living human beings are expressions of a creative purpose which cannot be fulfilled unless they abandon themselves to its force and intention: such abandonment as may be seen in the world outside man—perhaps most easily in the communities of ants and bees, or in the ascertained movements of the universe, whether in the solar system or in the atom.

Man as such appears to have in his make-up the power to decide things for himself in an area lying outside the working of natural law and the free working of instinct and heredity. He can express the creative purpose or obstruct, perhaps even destroy it.

The Christian interpretation of this is that men are fellow workers with God endowed with creative power but given the option whether they shall use it or not. Thus they can construct the institutions of humanity in such a way that they become new revelations or expressions of the divine purpose, or contrariwise that they become an obstruction or a hindrance to it.

The vital question for men both collectively and individually is whether they recognize or refuse to recognize, so far as their intellect is concerned, the consistent working of a spiritual force, which gives power and direction to its efforts; whether indeed man can create anything worth while other than in the power of the Spirit.

It is easy to see that instinct and heredity, working unhindered, maintain the uniform expression of the lives of animals, as, indeed, of human beings, in that area of their lives which cannot be or has not been invaded by intellect.   It is at least reasonable to suppose that as the lives of animals are enabled to fulfil their purpose by instinct and heredity, so the mind and intellect of man is made creative by the Spirit which, estimated on the lowest plane, comes direct to him from the eternal purpose and, on the highest plane of man's conception, is God immanent in human life—not necessarily effective in every man completely, but in so far as he is 'tuned in' to record and express.

The whole recorded history of humanity is replete with this effort of man to find out, to co-operate with, to become lost in the Creator of his being—the source of his life.

For ourselves and for our own western people, life became beautifully clear and plain when Jesus revealed the person of God in terms of the human organism, and conscripted, as it were, all men for the army of his fellow creators in the area of human life and institutions.

It is not inappropriate, indeed it is natural, that the supreme book of our race, the Bible, ends with the vision of the Holy City coming down out of heaven from God, comprising an invitation or an admonition to all men, to take part in building the cities of earth on its most excellent and enduring plan.

So, finding ourselves teachers, or destined to be teachers, in this first half of the twentieth century, and in the morning of our lives, we feel we cannot help but do so: the urge to do something real, something worth while, and an insistent hunger for service working in and through us as part of us, of the real force, the *élan vital* of all creation.

The urge is real, the hunger is real, the work lies ahead, the City of God here on earth is not yet built.

There are innumerable cities of earth and it is impossible to exclude any human being from citizenship.   In one aspect a city is where two or three dwell together; in another, it is the whole earth—the creation of the glory and honour of the nations.   But for our present purpose—or for one realizable part of it—we must think of English life and of one specific type of creative worker—the teacher.

The three supreme vocations of men are parenthood,

teaching, and prophecy; if these are fulfilled adequately the forms of human expression will comprise, as the pieces in a beautiful mosaic, the complete and enduring city.

Any one who would fulfil any part, however small, of this trinity of vocations for the unified glory of human life must live dangerously.

Of all occupations that of the teacher in schools is the most dangerous and the most responsible — partly because the school as such is not based so fundamentally as the family or the temple, or even as the farm or the workshop. It has not so many natural supports.

We have not yet evolved the perfect school, or, if we have, it may be we have not recognized it as such: perhaps it is, of all human institutions, the one whose evolution in the line of ultimate perfection is most difficult to promote.

Here and there, sometimes revealed but more often in obscurity, we find, not indeed the perfect teacher, but the teacher who, sore let and hindered, is moving towards perfection.

Let us try to imagine one such—man or woman—but for simplicity using the term man in its generic sense.

Such a one indeed will not necessarily be conscious of his real power: one's assumption of virtue, prowess, or strength often tends to discount these qualities. It is better far that a teacher should not dwell on attributes or faults, but go straight forward in the conviction that real power is seldom recognized because it is constant and normal.

This may sound perplexing, for surely a man ought to examine himself and find out his defects. Even so, but when he acts he really will not be thinking of himself at all.

The strongest influence which any one exerts is often exercised unawares: the big things one does slip past unperceived. If he perchance diverts or converts a life, it is not always when he is out to do it, but when, casually, he performs an act right out of the deeps of his nature, where it is in unity with, or part of, the creative force.

The difference between a really educated well-informed man, and a clever uneducated man, is that in the one instance the knowledge and training have been absorbed in the whole life, and in the other it is confined to the head. Out of the one it flows naturally, out of the other with conscious effort, self-approved in vanity.

The work in hand will compel all the powers of our teacher on the road to perfect expression. He will not trouble about other work which he would prefer to be doing. Acting as an assistant, or as teacher of backward children, he will not attempt to blind himself to his defects by idly dreaming of a school where he is headmaster. Face to face with children, even the most unlovely, he will see with his inward eye their innate majesty, their splendour, and their wonder, and he will be content if awestricken.

If he, in accordance with the custom of these days, adopts a slogan, it will be a reverent and appealing 'to be,' not an impudent and clamant 'to succeed.'

In all his ways he will reveal the spirit of a little child, which is the source and strength of power, which makes knowledge alluring and training an unending rhythm, without which no man shall enter the Kingdom of Heaven, that Kingdom built in part of the true and real thoughts of men on earth.

Enough! Who can limn the portrait of the perfect teacher—who has ever succeeded in truly describing or painting the least of men, let alone the man who, fired by wisdom with sufficient knowledge for all his purposes, lives in the power of all that is?

Across the area of man's life, where all should be free and unfettered, man himself, in the debasing power of body and mind divorced from the spirit which alone gives it life, has scattered — has built up indeed — litter and rubbish, has stretched hidden wires, and dug pits of destruction. He has built slums instead of sweet dwelling-places, and his palaces have in proportion become hideous and artificial. In obedience to false or half understood ideals he has erected schools which in extensive system or intensive content fail to answer to the teacher's needs, which repress his noble aspirations; the *raison d'être* of their existence, the child, becomes depressed, his gifts atrophy, and he goes out into the world a dullard without self-respect or a pert cleverling, conceited and ill-balanced.

What hope is there then of the full life for the teacher. Surely he has access in his own person to the sources of power. Surely the witness of reality springs up continually, bursting its way through the rubbish.

Surely no teacher need ever despair if he can look into the unclouded and unafraid eyes of a little child. Take a gloomy view of modern life and modern schools if you will, but only in so far as by contrast it shows the illumined view; do not dwell too long in contemplation of the rubbish, but lift up your eyes to the hills, the mountains, the stars, and remember the glory of men and the pure strength of children.

Even so, the teacher must have a plan—a perfect school in a perfect city. It must be the best he himself can perceive or create—not any one else's plan. Such a one would be useless to him. Not indeed that he should not contemplate and absorb as much as he may and will of the vision of the City of God, as John saw it, foursquare and pure, or that he should refuse the aid of St. Augustine or Sir Thomas More, or even William Morris, Samuel Butler, or his own—really own —favoured living teachers. All that and more he should build into it, every beautiful and true thing that he, by the power of the spirit in him, may perceive with his mind's eye and his physical vision.

But make a plan he must. Let him look at it daily, and ever he will see it increasing in beauty, and ever he will exert unconscious influence in bringing it into being.

In steadily rising degree the individual life he lives will become more satisfying, more exciting, more happy, and at times, at least, he will feel the whole force of the spirit, and thank God that he lives in so splendid an hour, in so glorious a world.

His citizenship will be clear and his title to it plain. There is the city of his own individual life, 'Mansoul' as Bunyan called it. The ordering of it is in his own keeping. No man can say him nay. He can perfect it—make body, mind, and spirit into a unity, keep the battlements, bar out evil from without, and so make futile the answering impulse from within. Clear the streets of his being of rubbish, eat to live, read the high recorded thoughts of men, look on the pure, the beautiful, and true, and destroy impurity and ugliness by the shafts of light from his own eyes.

There is the school in which he will teach—an institution of the city of all men.

He will not seek to reform it aggressively, but just be at his best, which is what he naturally is, and when occasion offers, whether of word or deed, he will use it fearlessly for the purposes of his own ideal, remembering always that there are other citizens, and his one and only inviolable contribution is his own personality. If it is a bad school, if it is ruled by a narrow-minded headmaster, or an ill-conditioned, ignorant body of managers, or a parsimonious education authority, he will forget or endeavour to forget it, and strive eagerly to develop such opportunities as he has, and he will remember hourly the glorious privilege of having forty, perhaps sixty, little ones vibrating to the rhythm he generates.

There is the city or village in which he lives, and if humanly possible it should be where the school is. Claims will be made on him, apart from those of his friends and his family. He must answer them boldly, always in relation to the needs and demands of his supreme vocation. Any teacher who enters a sphere of legitimate action, such as party politics, to take an easy example, in such a way as to sap his teaching strength or divert his necessary interest, even but a little, is so far acting treacherously to the children he meets and who wait upon his words, his deeds, and his influence. After all, the place for the exercise of citizenship by the teacher, apart from the duties laid upon all, is the area of his teaching, not to attempt to determine the direction and aim of lives, much less to dictate theories and opinions, but to invoke the forces of wisdom and to utilize the material of knowledge, to purify and strengthen, along the lines of their development, the personalities of children or adults, as the case may be.

Even a teacher who weakens his work in what is called 'the interests of the profession' is choosing the lesser part.

E

O ye gifted ones, [urges George Borrow in *Lavengro*] follow your calling, for however various your talents may be, ye can have but one calling . . .; follow resolutely the one straight path before you, it is that of your good angel; let neither obstacles nor temptations induce you to leave it; bound along if you can; if not, on hands and knees follow it, perish in it if needful; but ye need not fear that; no one ever died in the true path of his calling before he had attained the pinnacle. Turn into other paths, and for a momentary advantage or gratification ye have sold your inheritance, your immortality.

If teachers only realized the native extent and intensity of their influence they would say: 'Who is sufficient for these things?' and the only answer they can ever get—of any use—would be: 'No man acting apart from the power of the Spirit.'

Just a few instances of worth. I could tell you of a man who has done much to reveal the beauty of life to men and women in English prisons, an educationist by profession, whose whole outlook on life was altered by a simple act of common courtesy shown to him at a time when he was depressed and lonely, and perhaps not very sure of himself—an act of whose tremendous consequences the doer was quite unconscious.

I could tell you of an ignorant boy of eighteen with no more than the compulsory education of the public elementary school, and faced with the prospect of blind-alley occupations, whom a few wise words of precept and encouragement inspired with a passion for knowledge and launched upon a career of research that may perhaps banish the scourge of cancer from human life.

I could tell you of a man—he is not a teacher—who, since the birth of his two children, has scraped together every penny he could to assist them, and others as well, to get the advantage of good teaching. He is the most poorly paid man I know in regular industrial work, but any educational cause is sure of his aid, though his children need the money—and he more.

I could tell you of a man of eighty, living near London, who, having amassed more than a competence in business, devotes his whole resources to helping as many people as possible to get good teaching.

Each of you will be able to recall others—citizens all. Surely for our citizenship we are compassed about with a cloud of witnesses.

As in duty bound I would call you, before I close, to your supreme task of encouraging in the city every opportunity for grown men and women to get the knowledge and training they desire—and when occasion offers stimulating them to rise up and demand it in power.

After all, the school depends largely upon the interest and understanding shown by adult citizens who are not merely talking about education, but striving to develop in their own persons.

So then in the urge and movement of humanity towards the City of God represented in the terms of this earthly life the teacher has a part to play of inexpressible and abounding importance. He must play it in his own being, drawing strength from the eternal creative force, translate it into the terms of the school, and so far as may be into the life of the city, but every child he influences is a citizen, and he may work through unnoticed and unremembered days for a mere pittance, but by unspoken influence, or mere gesture, or by ready sympathy he may send out into the city a great builder, and so life becomes justified, and so one day the cities of earth will be so related to the City of Heaven, that they will meet in all their beauty, and human life will be over its whole area what it is in many individuals, perhaps more than we know, in our time.

11. THE WATERS OF LEARNING

(On 2nd June 1927 this commencement address was given at the university of Pittsburgh, U.S.A., and is here reprinted from the *University of Pittsburgh Record*, vol. ii, No. 1, October 1927. The true nature of education is investigated, the members of a university are referred to as 'the waters of learning,' and the address concludes with a brief history of university education in the Old World.)

PITTSBURGH is, in the eyes of the great world, a symbol of human material achievement, and of the application of the accompaniments thereof to constructive educational work.

It is the city of rivers, by the side of which have been reared, aided by their currents, mighty mills of force.

This is not the occasion to seek out or even to examine the cause or reasons for its unique power, but rather to recognize it, and then proceed to discuss, however briefly, the forces which in Pittsburgh, as elsewhere in the cities of earth, are ever working not only to create men and institutions on the lines and pattern of man's true destiny, but to reveal, as the fabric and texture of life, all those aspirations and acts of men, which are vital and real, health-giving and inspiring.

Every city strives even in its earliest days to express in its institutions the human hunger for government, learning, and worship; and there comes a time in the life of all of them when the city hall, the university, and the church burst forth in witness to these fundamental needs of humanity.

No great city is ever built by wealth of material and accessibility of position alone, but by the power of spirit and mind expressed by fine men and women. The greater its natural advantages, the more intense its need for wisdom, for knowledge, and even for prophetic power on the part of its people. If this be lacking or insufficient, then the common life will become mean and vicious, the noble material of earth will be utilized in ugly artificial erections, and the whole activity of the city will contribute to the decadence and perhaps to the destruction of a civilization.

Assembled, as we are, at commencement, we witness to the existence of the urge for learning, and if at times the pure power of it may seem to be sore let and hindered by those who would divert it for the premature production of misplaced or ill-constructed material, yet its direction and purpose are sure, for it is in the power of the spirit—the creator of new and wonderful manifestations of the working of eternal forces in the world for the glory and happiness of the life of man.

There is in the world a unity of all real things. Learning is one wherever and whenever it is manifested. The single-minded pursuit and realization of it in this university of Pittsburgh, or by its alumni scattered throughout the world, is one with the same activity in universities everywhere, which have been, which are, and which will be.

Philosophers tell us that time and space are not in themselves realities. They are, rather, expressions of the underlying and ultimate verities, adapted to the present, but not necessarily permanent, conceptions of the human mind.

Be that as it may, it is certain that the learning of Athens, of Paris, of Oxford, of Harvard, and of what university you will, is one with that of Pittsburgh, itself created by them, and a creator among them all.

You men and women of this university are the heirs of all the ages, and are destined to enrich the heritage, if you but use it aright, in the clear unafraid confident spirit of little children, reinforced by the knowledge and training which are the instruments of the matured life.

Some thinkers, though perhaps on a lower plane than the philosophers we have quoted, speak as though there were no present, but merely a past and a future. Time does not stand still; and so it is difficult for us, amid the rush and bustle of our ordinary lives, to hold it up for a while, and consider the method and direction of our use for it. Every possible metaphor has been forced to pay tribute to the rich idea, if not fact, of time; the 'sands of time' run out, the 'forelock of time' is seized, the 'river of time' carries us on, and the 'money of time' supports us. But perhaps a more helpful attitude is that which views the insistent present as the only real. 'The only use of knowledge of the past,' says Professor Whitehead, 'is to equip us for the present. The present,' he continues, 'contains all that there is. It is holy ground. . . . The communion of the saints is a great and inspiring assemblage, but it has only one possible hall of meeting, and that is the present.'

In all aspects the educated man is one who uses time aright, who redeems time, and since time is unceasing, the process of education is unceasing also. After all, education is nothing other than the effort of the individual inspired by wisdom to absorb and utilize the abundant material and the permeating forces of the world for the purpose of creating reality in himself and around him, or as Bergson expresses it, of 'sharing in the process of creative evolution,' or as St. Paul before him, of creating together with God.

Truly the destiny of man is splendid. The destiny of all men and all women, for every type is needed, even of those whose brains work slowly, or of those whose intelligences are simple, for by making the best of themselves, they set in motion the power and the force which prevent the quick-minded and clever from making fools of them and of humanity.

Moreover, the test of the individual life, if there be any test applicable by the mind of man, can only be applied at its close. For only then will it be possible to have any perception of the highest point to which that life has attained; and the justification of life lies in its highest and purest achievements. The mind which grows and develops, slowly perhaps, but healthily and purely, may reach a higher level than the brilliant mind which deceives itself into a perception of unreal power, or fatuous contentment, and ceases to harmonize with the ever-insistent urge towards its full and complete use.

If only men and women could see their supreme importance to the manifestation of the whole abounding unity, they would, in joyous abandon, seek for knowledge and training, as the very food of their higher natures and the means of making human life on earth like to the life of those who throng the streets of the City of God, a transcendent vision of the divine prophet.

sophisticated animal of no moment, with no purpose except to seek pleasure in life, then look down the roll of the past, or imagine the rivers of learning and purity in the world and bathe yourself in their living waters.

Look down, I say, or back through the years of our modern western civilization, perhaps only a fragment of time in the long story of the world, but still full of noble teaching, wondrous achievements, and adventurous endeavour. Everywhere and always, far flung over the world, you will find men seeking to create reservoirs of thought and learning, which for us, at least, have their culmination in this our university.

Think of the prophets of Judah, searching out and thundering forth the will and judgment of God, and creating that torrent of living waters that were gathered together in a later age by those inspired by the teaching of Jesus, and made into that vast reservoir, the Bible, which is the main source of the healing waters of our race.

Think of the philosophers of Greece, constructing in their academic groves the torrents of thought, the cadences of which are the harmonies of the mind; of the lawgivers of Rome ordering a barbaric world, constructing an enduring society; of the early fathers who, refreshed by the floods of learning, in the power of the Holy Spirit lifted life on to a higher level, though but a step or two up the illimitable heights of human possibility, and propelled it a mere stage on the immeasurable river of human capability, a river flowing ever onward to the ultimate City of God.

The Dark Ages swept over Europe, the waters of many rivers were apparently wasted, and certainly obscured, but ever and anon the school of the Church and the schools of law and medicine were constructed, Paris for theology, Bologna for law, and Salerno for medicine, the archetypes of them all.

It is mainly to the great gathering of the waters at Paris in the eleventh century that we owe the reservoir of learning at Pittsburgh. Every scholar in Europe who could manage it turned his face to Paris when Abelard taught, and the waters of their learning burst into every land, but particularly into England.

*E

It was in this wise. Paris was a *Studium generale*; the term university as applied to a place of learning was then unknown. It meant, if it meant anything, a gathering of faithful people from all parts of that Church which strove to be above every nation. In 1167 there was a migration of doctors, masters, bachelors, and scholars. With all the fervour peculiar to the university of Paris, they sailed up the London river until they reached Oxford, where on the river banks the schools initiated by the monks and nuns of St. Frideswide flourished. Here they found rest for their bodies and food for their minds, and were enabled to maintain and develop their organization which is the basis of the Oxford schools to-day. In 1209, for reasons of strife and disputation with the citizens, a stream of scholars set out for Cambridge, then a port, which had perhaps already afforded shelter and opportunity to masters from Paris, although of that there is no certain record. In any case, Cambridge became a reservoir of learning, and when, hundreds of years later in the early part of the seventeenth century, some of the finest of her masters sought the New World of America, they took with them the ideas and plan of their university, and created, hard by the Boston river, a new Cambridge, which, with the College of William and Mary,[1] sent streams of graduates to build in state after state, in noble city after noble city, the channels, the reservoirs, and the aqueducts of the waters of learning.

You see them, this Oxford and Cambridge, keeping the mind of the English people free, adventurous, and unafraid.

In their turn they were reinforced by the current of spiritual effort which revealed itself early in the thirteenth century in the brothers of St. Francis and St. Dominic, and created such men as Roger Bacon,[2] a prophet in the field of natural philosophy, and Robert Grosseteste,[3] the master spirit of his age. All learning flowed to the heritage of the Oxford and Cambridge scholars, except for a time the learning of Greece and Rome, driven eastward by the barbaric hordes.

Not that the rivers of it were always free of the rubbish

[1] 1692.   [2] 1214–94.   [3] 1175–1253.

deposited by pusillanimous and self-seeking men, nor that the additions made to them were ever uncontaminated. Even so, the thirteenth and early fourteenth centuries were glorious in their histories. Oxford is for ever shamed in that she disowned Wycliffe, not of her own will, but because she yielded her liberty to the State, which acted at the behest of the friars who hated him. Henceforth for many hundred years, almost even to the present century, the rivers of her life ran in many of its stretches into marshes and shallows. After his death at Lutterworth, as the chronicler quaintly remarked,[1] 'lying as a hare oft hunted by many packs of hounds in his forme at last,' his ashes were scattered in a brook feeding the Avon. 'Thus this brook,' comments the same chronicler, 'hath conveyed his ashes into Avon, Avon into Severn, Severn into the narrow seas, they into the main ocean, and thus the ashes of Wycliffe are the emblem of his doctrine, which is now dispersed the world over.'

Yet in time of need the river of learning which flowed in purity and power through the academic groves of Athens, and was revealed more clearly than before by the discovery of manuscripts after the fall of Constantinople, was, by the efforts of Erasmus, More, and Colet, made tributary to Oxford and Cambridge, and as a result that rebirth of learning known as the Renaissance enriched the life of Europe, just, indeed, as later on in the nineteenth century the waters set in motion at Oxford by a Roger Bacon in the thirteenth century, and at Cambridge by a Francis Bacon in the sixteenth century, became swollen into a river of scientific investigation and research. In every university acting truly to-day, humanism and science are alike supporting one another and enriching life.

There came a day, as we have seen, when the waters of learning were carried to the New World, and there in a land of unparalleled opportunity they have assisted development, not merely in America, but in the whole world, of mental and prophetic power, and of the application of principles to human needs.

[1] Fuller, *Church History*, Section 2, book 4.

The universities of the New World, when true to their mission, are gathering places of the waters of learning, sending out streams of fertilizing power, which have kept a multifarious people, untrammelled, adventurous, and alert, until the day of their great opportunity, which although not yet, is surely near at hand.

Do not let me idealize too much; but it must be remembered that the universities derive their power to exist from the waters of the river of learning. There may be trustees, professors, and graduates who have used the universities wrongly, defiling their waters in the pursuit of alien interests or self-aggrandizement or of unjustified power, and such men apparently have found the barren success they craved. But it is not upon them that we should concentrate our attention, but upon those who have used the universities rightly in the power of the spirit for the welfare of man and the glory of God.

As earnests of their latent power, the universities continually reinforce and make effective prophetic and inventive minds, which in a whole range of mental, material, and spiritual activities have commanded and held the allegiance of the world. Faithfulness to such leading and teaching by the graduates of universities will enable America to enrich human life in a manner now undreamed of.

The big thing in the life of a nation is the spirit of her people. If that is working freely and magnificently as a dynamic force, then mighty buildings, mills of steel, and repositories of treasure make up a glorious vesture indeed to be worn with grace; but, if that spirit works enslaved and feebly, then buildings, steel, and gold become a burden and a reproach, the instruments of vice and destruction.

Equally so the spirit of a man is the light of his life. If it burn but feebly, then his steps are aimless, or else they are vigorous on a false and unsatisfying way.

There is a passage in one of your own novels which expresses this, and I say it to each of you:

You have courage. You have strength. You have inherent ability. You have hunger for beauty and divine discontent which the world needs more of. You have that great, indefinable, invaluable thing which the world calls personality

—your greatest asset. All life lies ahead of you. It's flooded with colour and sunshine. And you're 'leaping as a strong man to run a race.' Wonderful! Start that race. Start for the Higher Hill Top. You can do it. All you need is someone to believe in you. Well, maybe there are far more people believing in you than you've ever dreamed of. Keep faith with them, even as you've kept it so far with yourself. Be true to your high calling wherewith you were called. Everything which has gone before has been education. You have reached commencement now. Ahead lies the world—the battle-field. Go in with your strong heart singing.' [1]

And all light is derivable from the right use of the powers, physical and mental, inherent in every man. All truth, all courage, all strength proceed from the rivers of it, reinforced by all men of all time who have expressed such noble virtues.

But to each man his own work.

O ye gifted ones, follow your calling, for however various your talents may be, ye can have but one calling . . .; follow resolutely the one straight path before you, it is that of your good angel; let neither obstacles nor temptations induce you to leave it; bound along if you can; if not, on hands and knees follow it, perish in it if needful; but ye need not fear that; not one ever yet died in the true path of his calling before he had attained the pinnacle. Turn into other paths, and for a monetary advantage or gratification ye have sold your inheritance, your immortality. [2]

In his own incomparable manner Plato strikes at once a note of warning and of cheer.

He therefore who hath always been occupied with the cravings of desire and ambition, and who busieth himself wholly therewith, will of necessity have got all his notions mortal, and as far as possible he will become altogether mortal; nor will he fall short of this in any way, since he hath fostered his mortal part.

But he who hath earnestly striven after learning and true wisdom, and hath been fully trained and exercised therein, if he lay hold on truth, must, one would think, of necessity acquire an immortal and heavenly temper; nay—so far, I say, again, as human nature is capable of it—he will in no wise fall short of immortality, and since he is ever serving the divine, and hath the genius which dwelleth in him ordered aright, he must needs be blessed exceedingly.

Jesus asserted the same truth in the question asked by all the great teachers: 'What shall it profit a man if he gain the whole world and lose his own soul?'

So, then, to sum it all up. Commencement is a time when men and women face anew the majestic glory of their heritage. Happy are they if they determine to use it in power of their spirits, for the purification of their own characters; to hand

[1] William Dudley Pelley, *The Fog.*
[2] George Borrow, *Lavengro.*

on, to those who come after them, new creations of their effort instinct with the rhythm of reality, living water for the healing of man.

In the eyes of such this university of Pittsburgh in the United States will acquire new splendour, and the service of all men everywhere be a noble cause.

> I vow to thee, my country—all earthly things above—
> Entire and whole and perfect, the service of my love;
> The love that asks no questions; the love that stands the test,
> That lays upon the altar the dearest and the best;
> The love that never falters, the love that pays the price;
> The love that makes undaunted the final sacrifice.
> And there's another country, I've heard of long ago—
> Most dear to them that love her, most great to them that know.
> We may not count her armies—we may not see her king;
> Her fortress is a faithful heart, her pride is suffering—
> And soul by soul and silently her shining bounds increase,
> And her ways are ways of gentleness and all her paths are peace.

So wrote Cecil Spring-Rice on the eve of his departure from Washington and shortly before his death. The purity of his emotion must inspire us all.

It would not be fitting did I not close with an expression of my own happiness in sharing to-day with you your commencement, for I am convinced that there is a unity of all men, like that which we have asserted of learning. In a world at times apparently confused and divided, this unity is most easily expressed, and, I venture to think, realized, by the peoples of the United States and of the British Commonwealth who apprehend the true meaning and purpose of education, and who derive their strength and power directly from the rivers of learning which have their source somewhere in the universe beyond our ken. Perchance they flow from the holy heavens, the centre of the vast universe of God, the mysteries of which are steadily being revealed as an abounding unity.

12. THE POWER OF THE SPIRIT

(This forms Chapter I of *The Educated Life*, an essay which appeared in the 'Affirmations' series in 1928. The idea behind the series, which was under the general editorship of Dr. Percy Dearmer, was to provide brief information upon modern problems by writers engaged in various pursuits. This extract speaks of God as a fellow worker with men, and outlines the development of the spiritual experience of man. The necessity for more spiritual training in schools is urged; the whole field of elementary education is surveyed, references are made to Denmark and America, to Church schools in England, and to the future of religious teaching.)

THE Christian is certain that all true force and power in human life comes direct from God, and that He is present amid its operation, to enable man to make full and complete use of what is manifestly His creation.

It is this sense of the immanence of God as a fellow worker which gives to man his supreme power, and which, amid all confusion, reveals to him a way of life which, proceeding from the heavens, enables him to build in human life and affairs a heavenly way which is directed back to heaven.

The story of the spiritual experience of man as received by Christians is simple in its outlines. In the process of creation, harmonized as a physical being or as an animal with the forces of the natural world, God 'breathed into his nostrils the breath of life; and man became a living soul.' Thus, in all experience, so far as the mind of man can array it, he is different from all else existing, not by a shade of difference, but by a vast gulf. The majority of his characteristics can be read into, or have been perceived in, one or other of the innumerable species of life in the world, whether he be regarded from the point of view of a unit or of a society, but, even so, there is in him a majesty and a power which clearly is nowhere else expressed.

He set out on his adventure with natural powers shared with all created beings, but also with spiritual powers shared with the Creator. The story of his procedure is one of vacillation, now relying upon his mind and body, now turning to the spirit. Across the way of life there flash and burn men so inspired that they were regarded specifically as men sent from

119

God to recall mankind to its true steps and destiny. These were prophets who could discern the true, even when it was obscured by the false, but even they had hunger for the actual and permanent presence of God, not merely as in His heaven, but as revealed in 'human flesh,' and thereafter in His very self, present in the world of His creation. Their hunger was justified, for Christ became incarnate, and revealed God to man in the plain terms of His own nature, experience, and understanding. 'Perfect God and perfect Man in human flesh subsisting.' Henceforward the life of man was to be different. He was not merely the created being illumined and vivified by the spirit breathed into him, but he was to be, and is, the chosen temple of the Holy Spirit, not merely 'of God,' but God. For Christ ascended, lifting our humanity to God, and the Holy Spirit descended, bringing God to our humanity.

This is the simple story. It is the faith of the Christian. There is no need for us to discuss here the facts that this recorded experience has not yet been recognized as supreme by vast areas of human beings making their way to God, or that there are many who, having lived amid its ascertainable influence, reject it as a creation of man himself in his endeavour to find a reasonable way of life.

Despite this prevalent faith, there is, in these days, a tendency for our schools and colleges to concern themselves mainly with the material of mental and physical training. This is natural in a world which demands so large a measure of skilled effort and work; so large a measure, indeed, that it must of necessity take up a large portion of child and adolescent life, and at the same time demand specific and concentrated treatment. The insistent demands of English people for men of character tends to prevent this tendency from developing unduly, as it otherwise would.

Indeed, Christians may rightly acquiesce in this as definite constructive work which, in its true progress and development, would harmonize with Christian teaching, but they can only do so on the assumption that the power of the faith is so expressed as to reach independently, or with the aid of the schools, the whole population and, further, that the schools will admit and assert the necessity of spiritual training and worship even though they themselves do not provide facilities.

It must, moreover, be made quite clear that the mere development of physical and mental powers, leading, as it certainly does, to increased power of production of material and natural things, commonly called wealth, may prove to be an obstacle in the way of the satisfaction of human life and aspiration, indeed, may increase disputation and discontent.

In the light of this tendency and attitude, the business of Christians, as such, is to regard all instruction in legitimate matters as right and fit for recognition as part and parcel of man's effort for living in accordance with the will of God in the world. They must never be tempted to make an artificial or unnecessary division between secular and sacred. Everything that is in itself healthy and pure may be utilized to minister to the welfare of man and the glory of God.

The acquisition of knowledge, or the development of training, as it becomes a matter of common necessity, may pass as literally into the daily life of man as the actual processes of the production, distribution, or exchange of commodities, the areas of which are outside the immediate areas of the Faith, which must occupy the whole background of human life.

In all the matters of daily intercourse and interchange Christianity has exercised, and still exercises, a dominating influence in England. The teaching of Christ is the final court of appeal which, even when not resorted to directly, still justifies or condemns the actions of all men. It has moulded laws, determined social relations, and marked the boundaries which none may overstep without damage to themselves and their fellows.

If in our time the influence of Churches as such seems to be weaker than heretofore, it may in part be because much of what they have stood for has become part and parcel of life. England, and we naturally think of England first, is as a country and nation nearer to the Christian idea of a community than it has ever been in its recorded history.

Yet, in comparison with the great need, little has been accomplished. The burden lies heavy on the Churches to search the mind of Christ, and to set up new and higher standards in harmony therewith, even though it be through ages of obloquy and persecution. Year by year the work of translating the will of God into the terms of human life must go on. The city that is far off must be increasingly realized.

In the area of education, although it is only the lot of the specially placed or the peculiarly gifted to undertake heroic enterprises or adventure, yet there is constant need for simple daily faithfulness expressed through deliberate self-sacrifice to an accepted position. Every one who talks about the schools or universities admits the power of their spirit to be the determining factor of their excellence. No one is contented with merely intellectual achievement, however wonderful. Men shrink from the clever man who seeks to act in the mere power of his mind apart from the accepted spirit of his time. The schools which turn out men and women of character, inspired to use their minds as the instruments of their whole personality in loyalty to that spirit which is greater than themselves, are loved and appreciated.

The doors of the schools are in reality open, and Christian influences enter, even though sectarian teaching be excluded from an increasing number of them.

After all, it is not merely Christians who desire that schools shall harmonize with Christianity. There are, of course, many who are resolute that they shall not become sectarian, and not a few who resent their enforced share in supporting schools, by rate aid at least, in which sectarian religion is taught.

Even so, England is just, and the community as a whole has decided that if a Church, national or otherwise, has set on foot and endowed schools, it should be allowed to maintain them, with the aid of public money, provided that the children in them have a fair chance of benefiting by all those opportunities which make up at least an approved education. The classrooms ought to be healthy and well ventilated, the sanitation perfect, the teaching regular and good, and the school ought to fit into a system which is steadily striving to give full and complete opportunity to all pupils, whatever the social or financial position of their parents.

The Churches which are responsible for schools must be willing to spend money provided by their members, past and present, to make their schools as good as those which are provided and maintained wholly out of public funds. In fact, the schools of the Churches must set new standards of excellence at all costs, or they will diminish in number more rapidly than they are doing and ultimately pass into the pages of history. They must advance or be superseded.

This is a hard saying for many who, believing in the absolute necessity of Church schools, find themselves unable to raise the money for the maintenance, quite apart from necessary extensions, of the fabrics. The Church school-house of 1870 may have been well enough, but the use of public money for new and splendid schools, together with developing educational practice, has placed it in a setting which not infrequently reveals its inadequacy for all men to see. The Board of Education, which has it in its power to condemn buildings as inefficient, has adopted a uniformly reasonable policy, and has co-operated in facing these difficulties with the managers of the heavily handicapped schools.

In the schools provided by local education authorities, fortunately, the Bible is still the leading book, and Christian teaching is implicit. These are big and encouraging facts. There are, of course, no sectarian qualifications demanded of teachers. Their religion is not called in question; it is tacitly regarded as Christian.

Provided always that there is not too much vexatious disputation and that reasonable concordats are entered into when and where necessary, this state of things will remain in form and steadily improve in spirit.

The whole future of religious education in schools, however, depends not so much upon the maintenance of fabrics as upon Christians increasing their direct influence in the community. It should be their endeavour to inspire and, as far as possible, train their young men and women who are fitted to become teachers. The schools will always be Christian in general and in detail, so long as there is a due supply of teachers who are Christian in belief and practice.

It is probable, indeed it is often asserted, that the children in elementary schools are better grounded in Holy Scripture than the boys and girls in the older grammar and public schools. These are, however, of diversified type. Many of them are deeply rooted in the tradition of the Church of England. Those which are happy enough to possess a chapel of their own have an indisputable opportunity to demonstrate the unity of study and worship. Such opportunities are used to-day with increasing, rather than decreasing, zeal. In most schools public prayers are a characteristic feature of every day. But in all schools everything depends upon the supply of teachers which, it cannot be too often emphasized, is determined in nature and in quality by the vigour and faithfulness of the Churches.

In the last resort everything gets down to the responsibility of organized Christianity. If that is weak, religion in the schools will be weak; if that is strong, the schools will inevitably be Christian.

Nothing further will be said, in this affirmation, of the 'sectarian difficulty' in elementary schools, except perhaps a passing reference to the difficulties inherent in the conditions of the new type of central schools. If the treatment is judged inadequate, yet some treatment is essential. For our schools arose out of the Churches, and would have continued to do so if the Churches had been strong enough and wise enough to bear the sudden burdens imposed by the Compulsory Education Act of 1871.

The Churches won their victory in demonstrating the necessity of education for all, even though they did not fight immediately for it. Success came either too soon or too late, but certainly out of due time for them.

Whether it be true, or merely admitted as possibly true, that the educational system, as we know it, is the result of the effort of Christians, it lays a heavy responsibility upon them in the future. It is they who must seek to initiate or invent, to bring forth treasures new and old, otherwise there will be no development in the power to utilize in a right way the increased material resources of the community which are the result of their right action in the past. The more men have, the better they must be, or they will misuse things. Education alone can make men better, and education is an affair of the spirit. The educated man is one who can utilize material aright, and the laws of right use are ultimately spiritual.

Nowhere recently in the field of education has the influence of men who worked in the spirit been so apparent as in the provision of knowledge and training for grown men and women. In a sense adult education is a new experience, although no community has ever existed healthily without it. When the revivals of learning developed in England, boys and men directly, girls and women indirectly, were affected together; so it was at Oxford and Cambridge in the thirteenth and fourteenth centuries, and later at the time of the Renaissance. Moreover, those interested in the adventures of the mind have invariably evinced a tendency to draw together in groups. In such a way the Royal Society was founded in the reign of Charles II.

In even primitive communities the fact, if not the form, of adult education reveals itself. Colonel Lawrence himself regarded the coffee hearth of the Arab chief as the university of the desert.

Yet it is only of late that the machinery of instruction has been utilized by those who desire to reach out in hours of leisure for the knowledge and training which their gifts and interests suggest to them, and which cannot be secured in the course of their daily avocations, whether professional or otherwise.

In all this men who are indisputably spiritual have taken the lead, such as Grundtvig in Denmark, Vincent in America, Paton in England, and Masaryk in Bohemia.

The Danish folk high schools, which revivified a nation, arose out of Bishop Grundtvig's devotion to the 'living word' in the hearts of men. His stock-in-trade was first and foremost 'the Holy Spirit,' then the spirit of the north; these he brought to bear upon the spirit of his time. Aided by Kristen Kold, he seized the opportunities afforded by the prevalent conditions in agriculture, utilized the Scriptures and the epics of the earlier heroic age of this people to make fine men and women who returned to the Danish farm with that spiritual power which made the fields laugh, as it were, to harvest.

In the New World of America, where education has always had a recognized tribute of devotion, J. H. Vincent, a bishop of the Methodist Church, aided by Lewis Miller, a Christian man of business, attracted for the first time, in 1875, a few Sunday school teachers to the side of Lake Chautauqua to study during a summer fortnight the principles of the Faith and to learn the use of books. Fifty years later summer schools, not only in the United States, but in England and Europe, have become a valued and potent force in the education of all types of men and women, particularly of those who desire fuller opportunities than can be realized in the ordinary course of their lives, or who are anxious to refresh and recreate their mental and spiritual power. It was from Chautauqua that Dr. Paton derived the idea of the Home Reading Circle, and was inspired to that campaign for right reading which has done so much to enrich English life, and which, in view of widespread uneducated reading, is still sorely needed. Masaryk, the blacksmith philosopher, yielded himself to the spirit of Bohemia with its immemorial Christian tradition, and in the face of innumerable, and apparently insurmountable, obstacles, seized the opportunity when it came, and gave self-government to his people.

This reliance upon the spirit is not merely a view of life; it is an absorption of life. Even the mere conception of its most powerful aid transforms existence. The sense of an abounding eternal force working in man and for man creates new values, inspires confidence, and is a dynamic power.

Imagine the school or institution, if it were possible, that ruled out that which it could not reduce to formula or intellectual expression. It would be a dead school, or at best unsatisfying, tending to mechanize men and women, irresponsive to all that is best in life, cynical about self-sacrifice, with laughter like the 'crackling of thorns under a pot.'

Contrast it with the best schools any one may know, where the light of worship illumines the day, where there is an abiding sense of the immanence of the Holy Spirit of God, where the little that is known expands and increases, because of the sense of the vastness of the unknown, where everything calls to physical, intellectual, and spiritual adventure, and where all feel that they are members of one body and that life's noblest activity is to rejoice with those that rejoice and to sorrow with those that sorrow.

Lest we are tempted to think that this is too ideal, we may remember that wherever a gracious teacher is at work these characteristics become increasingly real, and those who learn go out into life with new and abiding vigour. Such teachers have existed in the experience of all except those who have been more than usually unfortunate. The literature of education abounds with their achievements. In fact, they have created and comprise all that is abiding in it.

Some may be impatient and place their hopes for schools on their power to spread, if not to create, knowledge; but their impatience is not justified, for the pupil who learns most in the long run is one who has a sense, conscious or unconscious, of his own importance only in so far as he is related to a living unity, who feels that his business is to interpret the spirit in the terms of his own body and mind, and who is not eager for himself so much as for that life of which he is a part, and which reveals itself to him in his fellows.

The end of education is joyous life for all men, shot through indeed with that inevitable sorrow of earth destined one day to be caught up again in the certain joy of heaven. Wisdom, knowledge, training, are all part of the matter, the spirit fuses them, and man goes forth on his quest and adventure, creating as he goes, making melody and song, 'redeeming the time' even in days that are evil.

13. AN INAUGURAL ADDRESS

(The World Association for Adult Education was founded in 1918. Its first world conference was, however, not held until August 1929, when this inaugural address was delivered. Humanity is described as an expression of creative purpose; the mission and purpose of adult education is dealt with at some length. The most perfect expression of man is to be found in the innocence and purity of the child, the task of adult teachers being to make the way clear for children. There follows a spiritual conception of true education, which should have no ulterior motives, but should seek to develop the power in man for the use and glory of God.)

The multitude of the wise is the welfare of the world.

I

HUMANITY is one. It reveals itself as an unfolding unity, diverse in colour, multitudinous in methods of expression, moving down the ages, an animate line of power, on a little earth, set in a far-flung universe.

Whence does it come? Whither does it go? are the unceasing questions of every man, to which many answers have been given; but about them all, except for digressions here and there, lies a uniformity of conviction that humanity is an expression of a creative purpose, and that life on earth is but a phase of experience, set in a greater life.

Be that as it may, one thing is certain: man individually and man collectively counts. Even in his little day he can affect profoundly the conditions of his life. Summing up all his powers, he can uplift to heights of peace and beauty the relationships which he bears to the phenomena of the world, and even to the universe. He can secure firm fellowship and friendship in his inward parts—that is within the area of the entire human race. Nations shall not war with nations any more, but by mighty effort shall conspire for the common good of all, until the glory and honour of each of them shall be living parts of a glorious pattern of unified humanity, fulfilling the visions of the prophets and the seers of all time.

At such a moment as this it cannot appear as other than indubitable truth, that every effort made by men and women to develop and express the powers inherent in them, by relating them to the material and phenomena of the world, through the acquisition of knowledge, the increase of skill, and the absorption of wisdom, is and shall be caught up in the fabric of human welfare.

There is little need to go further. The wise man lives rightly, corresponds with the laws of his being, and relates himself by the power of his mind and spirit to all else that he perceives or divines. In the multitude of his kind lies the 'welfare of the world.' To add men to the multitude, to confirm and strengthen them when in it, is the purpose of adult education, is the *raison d'être* of our meeting here.

It is an episode, if but a brief one, in the long-drawn attempt of man to take his due share and part in the continuing work of creation, which is, as Eddington asserts, 'not an event in the dim past.'

If this be true, then man, in his present imperfect, but potentially perfect, condition, must strive to find out a certain way to carry out the work of a perfect creator or creative force. We shall dismiss at once, for the effective purpose of our consideration, the idea that man is a mere expression of the effect of the sun's or other rays, playing on the material or forces of earth, destined to rise and burst as a bubble, or to move as animate material for a brief space before becoming inanimate, or the mere manure of other animate life.

The dismissal of the idea, however, renders immediately necessary the acceptance by man of extreme responsibility. His must be, what Lord Haldane, greatest of British adult educationists, so often designated 'the toil of the spirit.' Man, in spite of the limitations which seem to be imposed upon him, whether in his own nature, or by the phenomena of the world, must through laborious and baffling days strive without ceasing to acquire knowledge, express wisdom, in the power of his spirit struggling to free itself and harmonize with the eternal spirit.

He must never be conquered by the reflection that nothing matters in a world which has witnessed the decline and fall of civilizations; and which still maintains inchoate, imperfect, and ugly expressions of human life.

Down the ages, and to-day, men fail to do their complete work. The unwise have rioted, and their riot has defiled and depressed the serried ranks of men. Their failures to achieve their tasks, or, rather, to endeavour to do so, their sins, as such failures have been called, have been visited upon their children from generation to generation. Yet the majestic power of wisdom translated into the terms of the bodies and minds of all men has never been without witness. From every camp, hamlet, village, and city, over the whole earth, the incense of pure power passes, in lesser or greater degree, to the great focusing point of the whole. The earth renders its tribute through the far-flung universe to the incomprehensible Creator. Yet it cannot be doubted that the joyous song of earth is shot through and through with the notes of pain, failure, and sorrow. The supreme song is not yet lifted by the voices of the sons of men. The kingdom of darkness, which is the area of the misuse and misplacement of the material and force of this world, has not yet been conquered by the kingdom of light, that kingdom which seeks to range on its side every human organism as it develops on earth.

II

The greatest teachers have, directly or by implication, asserted that the perfect expression of man is to be found in the innocence and purity of the child. A supreme problem is thus propounded, which involves the attitude of all men towards knowledge. There is, however, no choice to be made or differentiation to be propounded between the attributes of the child mind and those of the matured thinker. They must be combined, but the child spirit, which is part of the supreme spirit, must, if it is to be fulfilled, remain the same throughout the years of adolescence, maturity, and old age—which provide it with renewed opportunities of expression.

As the writer of Ecclesiastes surveyed the humanity of his time, he declared: 'For in much wisdom is much grief, and he that increaseth knowledge increaseth sorrow.' It is the

age-old dilemma, that will only cease to exist when wisdom
has that completeness of range which will enable not a man
here or a man there to know her presence and to be led by her,
but all men.   The wise man in this life is far too often the
butt, if not the martyr, of fools.   As for knowledge, it is only
incomplete knowledge which increases that sorrow which men
must bear, as they relate their lives to the ascertainable facts of
earth.   Fullness of knowledge is fullness of joy: a joy that has
caught up and transformed sorrow.

Be ye as a child, is the noblest of advice, but, while remaining
so, exercise all your powers, the stronger body, the more pene-
trating mind.   Search for knowledge with increasing zest,
but wonder at all you find, as the child wonders at every new
thing it perceives, and sees in it a promise of greater wonders
still.

III

The mission and purpose of adult education is in the power
of the spirit of wisdom, which works as persistently and surely
as any force known to man, to bring all the powers hidden in
humanity to fullness of expression by the perfect working of
body and mind with all that so glorious a state connotes.

Man is set in the midst of phenomena and material.   All
the marvellous working of his organism must be in unison
with the forces, natural and spiritual, which eternally and unceasingly work the will of the power which gave them motion.
In so far as this has been so, man has been splendid.   It
is in the confident assurance that wisdom is ever pressing and
forcing itself through the rubbish and litter which unwisdom
has created that the hope of man lies.

Welfare is freedom from litter, a state of perfect living
which mounts higher and higher, creating in its rising the
things which are pure and lovely.

In every diverse place the contribution which man makes
must vary.   The riches of all are brought into the mighty
whole.

Thus it is that although the dynamic force of adult education
must be, and is, the same in the Far East as in the Far West,

in the desert as in the pastures, in the prairies as in the cities, yet the method of its expression and the fruitage of it must be as diverse as the environment. There must be no imitation, but a real living union of personality with the opportunities which indicate in each place an actual need of the whole.

As one nation contemplates the achievements of another, it must resist the temptation to imitate, but must search out its own way, driving its mind, in the power of its spirit, deep into the area of the sources of its being, and then proceed through its own tradition, determined by its own environment, to the point of its own expression. As the East contemplates the West, inspired by what in the West it approves, it must set out to develop the treasures of the East, confident that in the perfection of its own work lies the ultimate hope of unity.

IV

It is an adult education arising out of such conviction and method which will lessen the area of doubt which surrounds so many men in the evening of their lives, whether or no education is an unmixed good.

There has been, and is, far too much value placed upon mere knowledge as inherently good. Teachers have forced, or tried to force, specific forms of it into every human being willing to be, or forced to become, their victim. The knowledge consequently possessed by many is a burden, it remains an inert mass in the mind, which it may clog and spoil. It is as though knowledge were fuel, which must be burned by the flame of the spirit of a man if it is to be of use to lighten his own life and that of others.

The doubter is justified, if he is contemplating the work of schools and classes alone or the process of making men clever, but he must not confuse this with the unfolding splendour of the life of man, which is the direct outcome of his permeation by wisdom, and his consequent use of knowledge for the expression of the powers that are in him, and the development of his right relationship to the reality immanent in the lives of his fellow men.

In the light of this consideration of the matter, there is no need to consider the uselessness of that knowledge which enables a man to work his wicked will, which brings him to disaster in this life, and which, whatever the future life can bring him, leads but to judgment, perhaps to purging fires.

V

As things are, tradition and experience must play their part with environment, even expressing themselves in what is apparently entirely new, in re-evolution as well as in evolution.

No people can escape their past, inevitable as it is. They must use it in the living present, the glory of the present to be, moving on in the mind of man to a limitless future.

The present contains all that there is [writes Professor Whitehead]. It is holy ground; for it is the past and it is the future. At the same time it must be observed that an age is no less past if it existed two hundred years ago than if it existed two thousand years ago. The communion of saints is a great and inspiring assemblage, but it has only one possible hall of meeting, and that is the present. The mere lapse of time through which any particular group of saints must travel to reach that meeting place makes very little difference.

It may be that time and space are illusions, created by the human mind to meet the temporal needs of the human organism. If indeed it be so, then every moment and every place justifies the supreme effort of Everyman, who is thereby destined to be in every thought and act everywhere, always.

Yet the act in present operation interests and holds us more than those long past. The same is not so true of thought or expression. It would seem that actions and thoughts are on different planes. That upon which thought is lies closer to reality than that upon which action is. A noble thought recorded or expressed endures in our experience thousands of years. Surely it is reasonable to believe that that which gave it motion, or of which it is the pale expression, endures for ever, far removed from the accidents of human life.

It would seem that if we would deal with things aright we should reject any idea which does not deal with the human personality in its entirety. As we have seen, there can and ought to be no division between the child and the man.

Yet there is no need to do other than admit the truth, for by doing so the way is opened for the consideration of thoughts and actions peculiar to the respective stages of existence. 'When I became a man I put away childish things' because they had accomplished their work in me. Thus we are justified in thinking not of education in general, but of the education of grown men and women in particular.

VI

It is imperative, if education is to do its perfect work in relation to infants and children, that grown men and women should, in and through their own persons, express it continuously.

That feeble conception of education which has been unthinkingly held, by many Englishmen at least, as a process ending as schooldays end, has been an untold hindrance to the development of adequate schools and scholars. Only those who are pursuing education for themselves can value rightly, or lead, the education of children. In the early days of the Workers' Educational Association in England its pioneers were urged to concentrate upon children, and leave adults, presumably past hope, to themselves. Their answer always was that it was precisely because they desired better education for children that they made adults their objective.

The supreme task of men and women is to prepare an environment for the children in which they can develop happily and in strength—to make a clear way for them.

If men and women cease to apply themselves, then the way of childhood becomes blocked with litter, and depressing, even poisonous, vapours damp down the rising fire of their spirits.

VII

As men face these great issues in the light of their experience and of the facts which surround them, they can only hope, and continue to hope, because of the truths revealed to them.

Any thought of man in the true line of his being is a direct contribution to the reality of a world still in the making. In less degree, because it is the consequence of his thought, every act in correspondence with the laws of life and nature also makes its contribution. It is because of such thoughts and acts, all down the ages, that the world is as it is. In all its tremendous fabric, the unity of an incomprehensible number of motions, it is a thought of the creative mind. As for man, evolved upon it, a fellow worker with the Creator, he has life given into his own keeping. Although he cannot affect the supreme facts of his existence, yet he can spoil and sully his body, his mind, his work; and he who does so damages all else whatsoever.

Adult education is a supreme effort to lessen the area of spoliation and to occupy it with the forces of redemption. It is in the line of the age-long purpose.

That reality, following the eternal law, is only achieved by correspondence with the underlying reality; it draws its strength, not from superficial actions or methods, but from the deep springs of the spirit. Those who would further it must not, in the first place, occupy themselves primarily with devising methods and institutions or arranging content, but in striving to become channels for the free-flowing wisdom of the universe.

In all the activities or work of man, it is the spirit which giveth life. Anything which men classify as great, be it gymnastic, art, music, poetry, or mathematics, is identified as such because it reveals itself as the free way of the spirit. That which our senses identifies has been modelled by mystic power. The material of the world has once more been caught up into the stream of creative purpose.

Only by such recognition will adult educationists be able to do beneficial and lasting work, which will arrange and express itself in such ways, utilizing such methods as the most discerning practical or realistic minds will be able to see and to approve, and the most ordinary minds be justified in reproducing.

The recognition of underlying forces is the secret of all great educational construction, as indeed it is of all religious systems. 'Seek ye first the Kingdom of God and His righteousness, and all these things shall be added unto you.'

VIII

All the great and abiding educational institutions of our western world have been conceived in the spirit which enjoins, indeed forces, men to seek for knowledge as for hidden treasure. They are the result of the realization that the human life of man depends upon his power of relating himself to everything that moves in the universe, whether it be the forces of nature or the organisms and material which they give rise to.

This process of relation is a great and glorious conquest. The mind of man moves back down the years, forward into the future. It strives to penetrate unending mysteries. Here at one time, there at another, because someone or other has worked in the spirit, he has discovered laws and harnessed forces to do his will. But the battle is in the morning of its day. Man knows so little. Perhaps in this life he will never know all. Certainly he cannot if he limits his powers by the possibilities of his senses and intellect. The big things lie in the area of the spirit.

The schools of Paris, Cambridge, Prague, Berlin, and Boston all bear witness to this truth. The East confirms it overwhelmingly.

As for adult education itself. To take only three examples, the high schools of Denmark were inspired by Grundtvig, the apostle of the living word in the hearts of men; the *sokols* of Czechoslovakia were conceived in the idea and spirit of liberty; the Tutorial Classes of England were projected to meet the spiritual rather than the intellectual hunger of men and women who had had little or no opportunity.

It is because of this dynamic force working through them that the actual methods ascertainable by expert educationists have succeeded.

Every one knows that new educational creations are at their best in their early days, when they are expressed by those who care for the essential things in them rather than for fleeting success. The day arises, sooner or later, when quite ordinary men, anxious for little other than remuneration and honour, enter them. As a result they become clogged with artificiality, that is, with work done apart from the spiritual motive. Life departs from them. Their remains must be cleared out of the way. That is why a reasonable function of many true educationists is that of scavengers on the mental and spiritual plane. It is their part to remove litter from the way of life, or from choking the wells of living water.

Because universities have dedicated themselves to truth, and were in their origins deeply rooted in reality, they have never entirely lost creative power. They never will whilst a sufficiency of men enter them in single-minded devotion to learning. The love of learning is an attribute of the spirit, and by its exercise men and institutions are renewed again and yet again.

This explains the perpetual power of our older English universities, founded nearly eight centuries ago, which, in spite of vicissitudes appearing to obliterate their real activities, have never let fall the torch of learning which they are privileged to bear.

In the present day they are sore beset. Demands are made upon them that they shall serve existing industrial, technical, and social needs. Quick returns, and plenteous at that, are stupidly demanded of them. If they keep the spirit of worship, and serve disinterestedly the cause of truth, refusing to be deflected by superficial demands, the springs of their power will continue to flow freely.

IX

All the great fundamental discoveries have been made by men who cared little or nothing for practical results. The immortal example of Faraday, out of whose work have arisen all the marvellous applications of electricity, is well known to the world.

The true researcher into the causes of disease, even, cares little, as he works, for the alleviation of the pain of the world. He does not confuse his mind with promises of so splendid a

F

result. His single-minded devotion to the truth for which he searches serves the ideal, the relief of pain, with greater power than if he had made that his objective rather than the search for the underlying operation of germ or non-living substances. Back to reality is the instinct of his life; it reveals itself in his work, to the results of which, be he successful, all things are added. Indeed, he cannot be wholly unsuccessful, for from all his work facts emerge, and not only facts, but the power of the efforts. Science itself 'has been built up on errors.'

In harmony with this, the true adult educator cares little for any ulterior motive whatsoever. His business is the development, through exercise, of the power of man.

He cares little for even such a noble thing as the development of citizenship in its power to run the modern state. As for propaganda in the interests of parties or institutions, such a process never enters into his consciousness as an educationist. He would admit that there are times and places for such effort. He may, indeed, at other times participate in it. He would rejoice as he contemplated developed citizenship, seeing in it the evidence of the soundness of the work of the educationist.

Get life into men—glorious life—through the exercise of their gifts and faculties, then they will relate themselves to their fellow men clearly and well. 'The knowledge of a wise man shall abound like a flood, and his counsel is like a pure fountain of life.'

Thus it will be seen that every legitimate activity of a man is material for his adult education. What that activity is and shall be, it is for the man himself to choose. In this connection I like to think of the rebellious temper of John Hunter, the great eighteenth-century comparative anatomist. He entered St. Mary Hall, Oxford, at a late age, knowing what he wanted to study. 'They desired that I should stuff Latin and Greek,' he said, pressing his thumbs on the table, and: 'These schemes I crocked like so many vermin as they came before me.'

Men tend, however, to choose in groups. The influences of time and place unify desire. Unique individuals either plough a lone furrow or create disciples who themselves form groups.

The adult educational effort of our time has emphasized the work commonly associated with schools — economics, history, literature, philosophy, sociology—though not unduly, because so many men who have interest in, and gift for, these studies have had little or no opportunity.

If the work goes on until the bulk of those who possess these interests are satisfied, then there will be no need to emphasize them.

Only a proportion of men and women have instincts and powers which need satisfaction through scholarship. The majority of them need simple instructive work, set in a decent environment which enables them to live, to love, to worship: which things comprise the whole duty of man, and to which all else is subsidiary.

There is a tremendous eulogy by Carlyle of the most educated man he ever knew, his simple, unlearned father. Few of us have failed to admire, with all our hearts, someone or other who, in days of simple unlettered toil, has attained to a serenity and beauty of life which is evidence of heaven's presence here and now. It has been my privilege to know several such, a gardener, a labourer, a railway worker. One at least of them knew no books: he read, and it sufficed him, pages of the book of nature and the faces of the fellow men he loved.

X

It is to our encouragement that we remind ourselves that many great discoveries and much creative intellectual adventure must be placed to the credit of men who have not earned their living by the work they pursued so passionately in their hours of leisure—men who have been termed 'amateurs.'

Such men founded in the seventeenth century the leading scientific society of England, known as the Royal. Every one of you will think of instances in your own country. There spring to my mind Cavendish, who established the great laboratory here; Gilbert White, the parson naturalist; Hugh Miller, the stonemason geologist; Barnard, the hatter microscopist; Bradley, the clerk philologist; and so on. These men were adult educationists *in excelsis*.

They and their kind keep the spirit of learning pure. They are more numerous, in a healthy country, than is commonly supposed, but they do not lend themselves to statistics and seek no publicity. All their joy is in their study. They remain contented and unnoticed, their discoveries often ignored, if not despised, because they are outside the artificial circles of professionals, too much infested by men who desire fame and honour, though that matters little so long as what they do is built into the fabric of the whole. Moreover, it often happens that discoveries and advances are made simultaneously by men set widely apart. 'The spirit bloweth where it listeth.'

If the 'amateur' is fortunate he may find opportunities in connection with universities, just indeed as Bradley, the clerk, did at Oxford, and Okey, the basket maker, at Cambridge. But there is another side to it. In the English and American universities I have had experience of scholars, men of science and of the humanities, who could have been offered, or who could obtain, enormous salaries in the world of business, but who continue on modest pittance to serve learning.

Big men in the business and manufacturing world could tell, if they would, of the temptations they have placed before university men in almost every powerful country.

The adult educationist thus must hold a special brief for 'amateurs.' In the increase of such lies the power and glory of learning. They construct the seed-bed of opportunity for 'professionals.' It might safely be said: 'No amateurs, no professionals.' If we think of adult education in what England believes to be its chief aspect for English men and women, as the attempt to restore or create the balance of life, disturbed by professionalism which must often inevitably weigh too heavily, it follows that 'no adult education, no education.' Truly the conception of adult education does not wane but wax in splendour as we meditate upon it.

It is so broad in its nature. There is, and can be, no activity of the mind and body of man which can be ruled outside it.

Divisions between mental and manual, technical and non-technical, reveal themselves as purely arbitrary and determined only by the condition and intention of the man making the approach. Nothing real is too insignificant to contribute to the education of a man.

Following this, the argument may be advanced that, when all is said and done, adult education is synonymous with living rightly. This is indeed its end and purpose. Even if it be intangible it is noble. The taunt was hurled at the English advocates of effort in the early part of this century that they had created an association for making people good. They were unable to answer it, other than by acting as realists in the power of their ideal, which it was their nature to do.

It was because they had an ideal so broad that they generated power to unite industrial workers and scholars, universities and Labour organizations, for the purpose of devising and constructing definite attempts, in a system or otherwise, to arrange facilities for groups of students, or for isolated individuals, to pursue courses of study or training adapted to their various needs and in accordance with their own desires.

As for the Government of England, working through the Board of Education, it accepted at the outset that such an ideal, faithfully held, would bring about definite results, upon which public money could rightly be expended. It co-operated at the outset.

. . . .

It is in private duty bound, and indeed as you would expect, that all I have had to say has arisen out of the English mind and experience of my own person, but I can say truly that I rejoice in, and have gained inspiration and knowledge from, many countries. The gallery of my adult education saints is filled with men and women, both past and present, far and near, who have done mighty works. You here will tell of some, if not all of them, in so comprehensive a conference, and reveal others whose fame is so far hidden from us. You will also speak of the new possibilities arising out of new material, of the wider diffusion of books, of radio, of cinema, of gramophone, of facility of movement, and place them in their right relation to the enduring needs of man.

In such a way, by such means, this unique conference will surely fulfil its work.

I have sought simply to speak of the underlying spirit of it all, of wisdom—of knowledge—of the unfolding splendour—which must be when these great forces and factors in the life of man are fused in harmonious power.

Sursum corda—Lift up your hearts. There can be no failure. The way may be difficult, long years may be spent upon it, but every step forward increases 'the multitude of the wise, the welfare of the world.'

14. THE DEDICATION OF LIFE

(This, the second annual Haldane Memorial Lecture, was delivered at Birkbeck College, University of London, in May 1930. After tribute has been paid to the work of the college, personal impressions are given of Viscount Haldane. His contribution to adult education, and his deeply spiritual life, dedicated to the service of mankind, are given special significance.)

ALL that remains of the human frame, or 'envelope' of his life as he would have regarded it, of Richard Burdon, Viscount Haldane, president of this college, 1919–28, lies in the beautiful burial ground at Gleneagles, hard by those of his family who had passed away both in times of peace and of war.

In the midst of the mountains he had loved so well, with lamentation of pipe and voice, a sorrowing throng expressed, as he was laid to rest, the soaring aspiration of his life:

> I to the hills will lift mine eyes,
> From whence doth come mine aid.[1]

It is in further memorial of this 'great servant of the State' that our words are dedicated this day.

'By the blessing of the Lord I profited,' he could have said with the son of Sirach, 'and filled my winepress like a gatherer of grapes. Consider that I laboured not for myself only, but for all them that seek learning.'[2]

I

As in private duty bound, I must first pay tribute of gratitude and devotion to Birkbeck College, in the University of London, and pray that it may flourish increasingly in these days of its unfolding life; that it may never cease to help men and women to live in dedication to high and noble purposes; that the records of its life to be, in Bloomsbury, may be worthy of the traditions set during a century in Fetter Lane.

[1] Psalm cxxi. [2] Ecclesiasticus, xxxiii. 16, 17.

The concluding words of the first Haldane Memorial Lecture, as uttered by Lord Sankey, were:

The world is all before us where to choose, and our joy no man taketh from us.

They would form, were one needed, a fitting inscription over the portal, or on some wall, of the new college.

'Birkbeck,' as it was known to all and sundry in the days of my youth, was an alluring place of knowledge and sound learning, dedicated then as now to those whose opportunities lay in the leisure afforded them after daily work.

I was myself a student within her walls in the early nineties —an elder brother had led me there. No one could have entered her gates with greater respect and veneration; but such was the rigour of my working days, and so diffuse the interests of my mind, that, although elementary Greek, chemistry, and political economy were the objects of my quest, I achieved no success that could be recorded in the books of the college, nor indeed in any other books. Yet, in so far, I am one of her sons, proud to come back to her for a brief hour, to speak words in praise of, and in service to, the work of that man of high purpose who was her president.

In common with all those who have sought to serve the high cause of adult education, I owe a debt of gratitude to Dr. George Birkbeck, founder of the college in 1823. He was the supreme constructor of facilities for working-men students in the early part of the nineteenth century. His works do follow him. Lord Haldane was, in many respects, his counterpart in the early twentieth century. Dr. Birkbeck, university teacher as he was, planted seeds of university colleges, whilst Lord Haldane nurtured the resultant trees and helped them to fructify.

With Dr. Birkbeck in the background and Lord Haldane as a living exemplar and teacher, it was my privilege to set out in 1900 to endeavour to widen the field of opportunity open to those working men and women who were, or ought to become, students. Almost the first words I wrote in advocating the formation of what was to become the Workers'

Educational Association were caught as they fell from his lips when addessing Scottish teachers in December 1901:

Educate your people, and you have reduced to comparatively insignificant dimensions the problems of temperance, of housing, and of raising the condition of your masses.[1]

Almost from the outset of the work of the newly conceived association he, realizing, as few men then did, the necessity of higher education for working men and women, became a consistent and generous supporter, a stand-by in trouble, an opener-up of opportunities, and a stimulus to advance.

During the weary years of the Great War, seizing the opportunity, he planned and schemed for the advance of education, with that purposeful concentration which characterized his work in time of peace for the better organization of the army against a day of unhappy need.

Those of us who had continuous and occasional chance sat at his feet. He became, to us, a Gamaliel.

To me he was both generous in counsel and overflowing with inspiration.

The knowledge of a wise man shall abound like a flood, and his counsel is like a pure fountain of life.[2]

For him, I admit unhesitatingly, I have no criticism.

Fallible he must have been, as indeed are all the sons of men, but he moved serenely on a plane of devotion to, and appreciation of, learning and knowledge, dedicated to high purpose, which, as I contemplated it, filled me with veneration to the exclusion of all else.

Of the details of his life, so far as he has revealed them, it would not become me to speak, for that opportunity fell to Lord Sankey in the first Memorial Lecture.

Mine may be, I am bold to think, the occasion to consider the passion of his mind—expressed in intense desire that life, a phase in the existence of man, should be dedicated and re-dedicated, in the power of the spirit, to high and noble purpose: to consider it in my own way in the force of his inspiration, and

---

[1] *Education and Empire*, p. 39. John Murray, 1902.
[2] Ecclesiasticus, xxi. 13.

to reinforce my consideration as far as may be with his actual words.

The manner of his own dedication may then be contemplated. Such consideration and contemplation may not unfitly be prefaced by some personal impressions of him.

II

Lord Haldane has been described as inscrutable, but in the eyes of those who knew him well he appeared as the most simple and human of men; in spite of the fact that behind the ordinary amenities and courtesy of his expression lay, most certainly, the currents of masterful, undeviating purpose.

He was the strong man, gentle. In this he was true to the characteristics of his own people. Observers have noticed the gently expressed strength in more than one member of his family. Perchance it was derived from that deeply religious man 'of an old-fashioned type' who 'loved a simple country life'—his father; as also from that mother who was 'gentle in her relations' to her children but always endeavouring, and who shall say not succeeding, to bring about what she believed best for them. She was, so he himself tells us, the 'dominating influence' at Cloan. Until her hundredth year her splendid personality grew in outlook and in spiritual insight. There was no tendency in her to exercise restraint on others. Sometimes I wonder if there is any sentence more beautiful in its implications, written in any autobiography, than this: 'I wrote to her every day from 1877 down to her death.'

He that honoureth his mother is as one that layeth up treasure.[1]

In the great world groups of young lawyers, young philosophers, young politicians, young educationists, must have been strengthened in their purposes by his wise and gentle counsel. The picture was drawn for me, only a few days since, of the patient happy way in which he sat for hours at the early meetings of the now powerful National Council for Social Service, helping to discuss details and to formulate

[1] Ecclesiasticus, iii. 4.

plans of action; not seeking to dominate or to impose his views but, as an equal among equals, both giving and receiving.

Like all truly great men he was ready and eager to lay his mind side by side with the minds of others. No one he naturally came into contact with was too insignificant for him. He conferred equality upon them by the uplifting power of his own presence.

There was about Lord Haldane an atmosphere of complacency. Superficial observers failed, indeed must have failed, to realize its true meaning and significance. It arose out of the confident certainty, so continuously his as to be habitual, if not subconscious, that his real personality was deeply rooted in the spirit. He was, as a direct consequence, detached from that world in which he was playing a man's part. The rebuffs and contumely, as well as the welcomings and praise, of his contemporaries could only affect the outer envelope of his life.

One of the many amusing tales told of him was a caricature of this characteristic. In the days of Moody and Sankey, passionate messengers of salvation, on an occasion he was at a reception to them. As was the wont of Moody, at least, the guests in turn were asked the searching question: 'Are you saved?' But to Lord Haldane, standing with his back to the fire calmly surveying the scene, Moody could only say in veneration: 'I can see it is all right with you, brother.'

In spite of his varied interests he limited himself in the face of a task to be accomplished; whether it were in philosophy, or law, or politics, or education, he made it 'whole time.' This can be seen, clearly enough, in the record of his life. He never dissipated his power by turning haphazardly from one thing to another.

'If a man would succeed he must be a whole-timer,' he once said to me, and he illustrated his assertion by references to the lives of great politicians who had held the office of Prime Minister. Those who had allowed other interests to invade unduly the area of their work, in so far as they did so, lost their continuous grip or floundered. The dedication of life must be to a main and compelling purpose; all other things must subserve it.

The first duty of life [he counselled students at Edinburgh[1]] is to seek to comprehend clearly what our strength will let us accomplish, and then do it with all our might. This may not, regarded from the outside, appear to the spectator to be the greatest of possible careers, but the ideal career is the one in which we can be greatest according to the limits of our capacity. A life into which our whole strength is thrown, in which we look neither to the right nor to the left, if to do so is to lose sight of duty—such a life is a dedicated life. The forms may be manifold. The lives of all great men have been dedicated; singleness of purpose has dominated them throughout. Thus it was with the life of a Socrates, a Spinoza, or a Newton; thus with the lives of men of action such as Caesar and Cromwell and Napoleon. . . . They may have perished before their end appeared accomplished in time, and yet they have succeeded. The quality of their work lay in the very striving itself.

Lord Haldane viewed with concern the increasing tendency, in a highly differentiated world, for men to try to do, not only too much of too many things, but, because some of them were authorities on one thing, to speak as though they were authorities on others. Yet, of course, he was never the apostle of narrow specialism. After all, life is broad and must be viewed largely. He would have appreciated the dilemma expressed by John Burnet, his countryman, in the Romanes Lecture of 1923:

It seems that the more there is to be known, the less of it can we know, so that the growth of what, for any one of us, can only be potential knowledge is necessarily to the same extent a growth of actual ignorance. Our knowledge bears a diminishing proportion to the mass. . . . We are told, to be sure, that specialism is the remedy. . . . There must be something wrong here; for this system, if pushed to its logical conclusion, would land us in a society where no one knew anything that any one else knew.

His constant endeavour, as he counselled the Association of Headmistresses in almost his last public utterance, was to attempt 'to get a grasp of what the whole thing means'— life and the dedication of it. In this we may follow him.

As he saw it the life of man is spiritual. Body and mind are but its changing and temporary vesture. Death belongs 'to what falls outside the inmost nature of the spirit.' The high privilege of man is 'to think and do work based on thought' so that our human nature may express itself with the

[1] *Selected Essays and Addresses*, p. 37. John Murray, 1928.

quality of truth, and so unfold in beauty to the fulfilment of the divine purpose. 'Our duty is to work without turning our eyes to the right or to the left from the ideals which alone can light up our paths.'

The man who has dedicated his life, the man of purpose, does not, need not, blind his eyes when perplexed or revolted by the ugliness and cruelty rampant in the world; but, conscious of the working of a greater plan, which he can only conceive or even imagine in part, proceeds courageously and therefore nobly on his own way. He strives to redeem such time as he is able, and in the striving finds happiness. All his powers and gifts he burns on the altar of his life and the burning purifies and strengthens them. As for death, come it early or late, it shall be unaccompanied by fear. He is above the event. All his good work remains—perchance also all his good, though unrecorded, thoughts—a possession of the race, so long as it is needed.

III

Dedication of life implies that a man must get a clear idea of what he believes, what he wishes to do with his life, and what he desires life on earth to be.

It is possible for every man who faces the problem of realizing these ideas to succeed in greater or less degree.

Moreover, the ideas will continue to develop as experience, and the interpretation through knowledge of experience grows.

'What we find is always developing itself and assuming fuller forms.'

'The toil of the spirit,' as Lord Haldane termed it, must persist throughout. It is the lot of all true, or dedicated, men.

Decisions governing immediate action must be made at the outset.

If belief is positive, and not negative, it has all things open to it. The mind of man is like a city into which all things may be brought and within which they may grow; the gates may exclude the undesirable if the spirit is awake, but alert it must be, for

> Man's Reason is in such deep insolvency to sense
> That tho' she guide his highest flight heavenward and teach him
> Dignity, morals, manners, and human comfort,
> She can delicately and dangerously bedizen
> The rioting joys that fringe the sad pathways of hell.[1]

In making such a momentous decision as that governing the use of life for the purposes of specific work a man is guided mainly by the gifts and capacities he discovers in himself. Such are sometimes the keys of opportunity. At other times they may be baffled, though never wholly prevented, in their attempts at expression. One thing is certain and that is, that if a man would live fully he must strive, and continue to strive, to express his gifts, no matter how untoward the circumstances. It is not merely a matter of 'getting a position.' It must pervade the whole of life. If a man finds no chance in a working day then he must make it in his hours, or even moments, of leisure. Only in such a way will he feed the fires of his spirit.

There are many men of whom it will be said foolishly that they have no gifts. Such, as a result, tend to become depressed. It may be true of them that they have no gifts which the passing world admires because of their rarity of expression, but at no time have common things been unnecessary, whilst at all times they have been most necessary. To paraphrase Abraham Lincoln: 'The Lord must have loved the common people. He made so many of them.'

So the discovery and expression of gifts and capacities must in reality be transcended by the idea of the full use of the creature. Moreover, it may well be remembered that the right living of a simple slow-minded manual worker may be the necessary prelude to the life of an artist or a prophet.

Man in the world, set in family and community as he is, must of necessity relate himself to the actions and opinions of those about him. Often they will seek, misguidedly, to let and hinder him; but, having paid, or continuously paying, his tribute of honour and respect he will, if he be wise, make

[1] Robert Bridges, *The Testament of Beauty*.

his own decision, and in so doing he will give most weight and leading to the movement of his own spirit.

In every good work trust thy own soul.

The decision having been made, the life dedicated, come what will a man must go ahead, unless fuller light reveals the necessity for re-dedication, in whole or in part; but for the greater part men can go right on.

After all, the highest contribution a man can make is the increasing or unfolding perfection of his own being. Be life long or short is a matter of less moment than appears at first glance.

> It is not growing like a tree
> In bulk, doth make men better be;
> Or standing long an oak, three hundred year,
> To fall a log at last, dry, bald, and sere:
> A lily of a day
> Is fairer far in May
> Altho' it fall and die that night;
> It was the plant and flower of light.
> In small proportions we just beauties see
> And in short measures life may perfect be.[1]

As his ideal for himself is translated into the actions of his life, so he gains a clearer idea of his desires for the life of men on earth; and he will indubitably perceive that the contribution of most men is made through their own thought and action, quite apart from the promotion of what is called social reform.

But this common life of man draws out all that any man can give. From all men it asks 'faith, hope, and love,' whilst it needs husbandmen, diggers, hewers, carriers, craftsmen, architects, poets, musicians, artists, prophets, and priests. If all men did their bit the whole would be beyond our imaginings. But if only one man does his bit he is justified.

Thus decisions can be made with confidence, even though men may be unable to discern clearly the truth about the meaning of life. 'Where Plato and Aristotle and Kant were not sure of their knowledge how dare we be?' asks Lord Haldane.

[1] Ben Jonson.

Yet he, the most practical of men, would urge that the dedication of life postulated a fundamental belief or conception.

The only question is whether what he chooses is of the highest quality. He practises the presence of God in his own fashion and in the shape that appeals to him vividly. It is by thus disentangling the higher implications of our experience that we approach to God.[1]

There are indeed those who regard our human life as, in some not yet understood way, the expression of a combination of the rays of the sun, or other rays, upon the dust of earth, destined to be what we call animate for a while, to live, move, and have being, and then to fall back to the dust again, material perchance for other animate life of a different variety, with, as final destiny, the steady or catastrophic destruction of the earth of which we are a minute part.

'I believe that when I die I shall rot,' says Bertrand Russell, 'and nothing of my ego will survive.'[2]   Yet he would approve, even demand, the dedication of life.

The good life is one inspired by love and guided by knowledge.[3]

The attainment of his good life, however, lies apparently wholly in the power of man, as such.

Science can, if it chooses, enable our grandchildren to live the good life, by giving them knowledge, self-control, and characters productive of harmony rather than strife.[4]

Lord Haldane for his part states:

That the more experience is spiritual the more it is real has influenced me through the course of life, during more than fifty years.[5]

The main postulates for the good life must be the same in all thinkers: the difference lies in the sources of power to live such a life. On the one hand, the human mind—on the other, the eternal spirit.

There is, and can be, no doubt that Lord Haldane regarded the human nature of man as an opportunity afforded him for a

[1] *Affirmations : Mind and Reality*, p. 21.   Ernest Benn Ltd.
[2] Bertrand Russell, *What I Believe*.   Kegan Paul.
[3] Ibid.
[4] Ibid.
[5] *Autobiography*, p. 348.   Hodder & Stoughton.

brief space to express, in terms of body and mind, the motions of the spirit—the power of God.

'God is not outside us, but is within our breasts—"an almighty, ever-present Deity."' 'This is a principle,' he said, 'we do well to make our own as early as we can in life and to keep always before our eyes.'[1] Rabindranath Tagore said, speaking at Oxford only yesterday:

It is this supreme person, this divine in man—so hard to define or name—in whom we live and move and have our being. All the prophets and poets and sages have pointed us forward to this inner unity of man, this spirit of love within, by living out the truth of it in their own lives.

'The fuller view,' which to Lord Haldane, if it did not transcend all Christian creeds, was an essential aspect of them,

has given me [he writes] a sufficient solution of the problems of existence and has taught me that it is not on how to die, but on how to live that one ought to concentrate. Death is in this view but an event which comes as the necessary outcome of the course of organic life. It belongs to what falls outside the inmost nature of the spirit. We do not pass out of an independently subsisting world with it: that world on the contrary passes from us and we can contemplate it as so passing and thereby we are lifted above the event.[2]

This fundamental conception of the abiding spirit and the passing world is in its essence harmonious with Christianity. He himself never attempted, in public at least, to extend it to the expressed dogmas of the churches, but he would have recognized as at least symbolically sound, based on an 'unassailable idealistic principle,' the communion of saints, the angelic company of heaven. His heart would have leaped to the unity of the worshippers' praise with angels and archangels. The saying of Jesus, that the angels of 'little ones do always behold the face of my father which is in heaven,' must have filled him with ineffable comfort.

The conviction that after this life he will still be explains much of his courage, justifying almost the last words he was heard to speak: 'A little tired, but all is well.'

Just in so far as men hold this conviction so indubitably human life will grow in splendour. Martyrdom and sacrifice inevitably become the sanest and wisest acts, not, as some think, the vain efforts of misguided lives. To such a truth

[1] *Autobiography*, p. 344.   [2] Ibid. p. 349.

the noblest and highest acts of men and nations in all time
have been fearlessly dedicated.   They are the reality to which
the hearts of men leap.   Yet no one saw more clearly than he
did that sacrifice and martyrdom must come in the inevitable
line of life.   To seek it or to court it were a fool's game.

Lord Haldane has bequeathed to us the memory of a man
firmly planted on earth, doing daily tasks faithfully, but de-
riving his power to do so from the immanent spiritual and
eternal.

Our life on earth is therefore an opportunity to work at, to
participate in, the work of creation—'a continuing process,' as
Eddington regards it, 'made possible by the application of
conscious mind.'   Such a realization is in itself an urge to
action.   It satisfies the needs of men.   The hither-whither
of life vanishes.   Every man is in the line of age-long purpose.
Dedication becomes the supreme act.

IV

In the consideration of the working of these principles in
the life of Lord Haldane it is not necessary for us to attempt
to estimate his place in the gallery of the great.   Even if we
possessed the qualifications for such an attempt it would be
but futile and artificial, a mere intellectual motion.   That he
was great in the ordinary sense of the word is admitted by all
but the prejudiced in his time and generation.   In the realm
of human affairs England is what she is largely because of his
gifts and prescience.   'Where would we be to-day,' asked
Earl Haig, 'without the imperial general staff which was
your creation?'   So might also ask any chancellor of any
newer English university: 'Where would we be to-day if you
had not sought to extend university organization in England?'

His work was of such far-reaching importance that it could
attract the vituperation of those who are ever ready to rail if
prophecy and action are not exhibited in the setting of
omniscience.   Does England suffer—then pillory someone!
Thrust him from his seat!   So they treated Lord Haldane—
politicians, press, and people—until the day came, as Haig

hoped it would, when the meanest of them was dumb and the best ashamed. Throughout it all, whether praise or blame, he lived, as always, above the battle.

Only the Master shall praise him and only the Master shall blame.

His Master dwelt in the retreats of his own mind and spirit.

On a fateful day, as he walked from the War Office to his house in Queen Anne's Gate, rejected from high office, the seals of it in other hands, he, knowing another service, that of the mind, was unperturbed in the innermost of his life. There, in his study, were the fragments of his written philosophic work waiting to be welded into unity, to appear later as *The Philosophy of Humanism* and *Human Experience*. In that room of his he was monarch, his subjects the well-stored, alert brain and the company of books ready to serve him. There, too, he could commune with his many friends. Subjects and friends would fill his days. No place would be left for disquietude, much less for bitterness.

He must often have recalled the lines at the beginning of the second book of the *De Rerum Natura* of Lucretius; it was indeed his habit to do so.

> But sweeter far to dwell remote, aloof
> In some high mansion built on Wisdom's hill,
> Thence watch the errant crowd go to and fro
> Matching their wits, striving for precedence,
> Toiling and moiling, hurrying night and day
> To rise to fortune and possess the world.

In very truth, that top-floor sanctuary of his at Queen Anne's Gate was symbolical of some high mansion on the immortal hill of wisdom.

The teachings, or rather the thoughts, of Lord Haldane, based on wide learning achieved through laborious days, are embodied in his many books, in which the student of philosophy will find detailed and faithful examination of the theories and assertions of the master thinkers, always regarded from the point of view of their application to the world of action as he perceived it. Their effect will be revealed in the outlook of many generations to come. Together with his published addresses they express no inconsiderable part of the constructive mind of England as it revealed itself in transition from an age of expressed ideals to an age of their testing. The solidity, complacency, and emotionalism of the Victorians had, in his later years, to face an influx of scientific discovery, an avalanche of mechanical and electric power, the crashing impact of world war, and such a ferment of unrestricted thought as might well be termed revolution.

He began in the old, he lived in the new, and he passed away in the certitude of those fundamental truths which have moved the hearts of men in all time and stirred them to work and action.

In the deeps of his life he was a man of all time. That is the secret of his abiding confidence and strength. Unperturbed by the changes around him he trod his confident way.

All this is revealed clearly in his addresses to students. It would seem that the opportunity to speak as Lord Rector to the young men and women of Edinburgh University on 'The Dedicated Life' stimulated his powers to the full. To such a one as myself, looking out to things in London, the address, as published, came as a message of confidence and hope.

Because his thoughts were his own and concerned with fundamental things, they recur throughout his writings and were revealed in his speech over and over again.

Of the 'larger outlook,' as he termed it, he often spoke.

None but the largest outlook can suffice for the discovery of the meaning of life or the attainment of the peace of the soul. It is not in some world apart that the infinite is to be sought but here and now in duties that lie next to each. No longer need men sit down and long for something afar from the scene of their toil.

'Peace of the soul' was to him, as we have seen, the supreme happiness of the dedicated life. It is to be achieved by all who devote their gifts and talents, through laborious days, to the accomplishment of a true purpose.

If we have striven to think and to do work based on thought, then we have at least the sense of having striven with such faculties as we have possessed devoted to the striving. And that is in itself a course of happiness, going beyond the possession of any definite gain.[1]

[1] *Autobiography*, p. 354.

The passion for excellence, the domination of a single purpose which admits of no intrusion, can suffice for him who would reach the heights.

When the passion for excellence is once in full swing it knows no limits. It dominates as no baser passion can, for it is the outcome of faith that can move mountains.

The distinction already drawn between his teaching and his thoughts is justified in that, though inevitably a teacher, he was content to be and to know. As occasion demanded he bore witness and was ever ready to step deliberately forward to do so. Of all things 'to know' was to him the highest— higher than 'to be.' 'I think,' he writes, 'I have in the main followed Leonardo da Vinci in the faith that it is better to know than to be.'

The urge to unify his being with truth and to possess the certitude of it in his calm and resolute mind was continuously upon him. His conviction was that so 'to know' was to be, himself, part of the eternal mind. Knowledge in itself was to him not merely erudition, but wisdom relating itself to the phenomena and force of the universe and rewarding man with the ascertainable fruits thereof. 'Now we see through a glass darkly,' he had no doubt of that—'but then face to face'— that was his conviction. 'Now I know in part, but then shall I know even as I am known'—that was his comfort. The passion of his life was to increase the area of 'in part' here and now—to know more and more. The conviction of his life was the comforting certainty of fullness of knowledge hereafter.

He was no mystic in any other sense than every man is bound to be. Visionary he certainly was not. He used his powers to the full, sought out underlying principles, built upon them, here a little, there a little, line upon line, and left no weak places. In short, he did that which came to his hand as the best and most complete preparation for what might be required of him hereafter. The service of his profession and of his country was carried out in fidelity to such a method.

In all his work 'detachment' helped him. It explains much of his power. If 'the world,' as he asserted, 'passes from us,' how much more completely do the 'toils and chances' of our lives pass. Paradoxically enough such detachment increased his organizing capacity. It enabled him to see the wood whole and saved him from running into trees.

Such a type of man as he was, ever looking to underlying principles, was of necessity in matters of belief bound to be lonely and apart. Just as, on a different plane, some men are unable to join a current political party because no one party satisfies their needs, so he was unable to be a consistent member of the church of his fathers, or of any church. Yet he cared for the churches. His belief in their necessity was intense. 'It would be an evil day for this country,' he wrote, 'if the churches ceased to function or if their function were diminished For to them is entrusted the maintenance of standards in life.' [1]

He never for one moment thought that the holders of creeds were limited any more than he himself was. For ordinary men creeds are the *pied-à-terre* of the religious life. All that he held was that creeds were, by their very nature, bound to be inadequate expressions of the overwhelming truth out of which they arise.

V

It is meet and fitting that we should glance in our own way at his attitude towards adult education. 'Much more,' he wrote in 1928, 'ought to be known about the new movement for diffusing adult education. It is a deeply interesting one and it is growing rapidly. It is attracting some of the finest spirits in the universities.' Our task is a light one, for the Lord Chancellor accomplished the burden of it in the first Memorial Lecture in an effective and complete manner.

Lord Haldane's ever-present interest may be traced in his interpretations of philosophy, law, and politics—to him a trinity in unity, out of which grew wise and instructed efforts to inspire lives dedicated to education.

At the close of the nineteenth century he admits that the

[1] 'The Churches and Higher Education,' *Hibbert Journal*, January 1928.

chief problem he had put before him was 'How to extend university organization in England.' At the zenith of his political career he regarded education as transcending party politics. 'I did not mind,' he admits, 'accepting the opportunity of throwing myself on Balfour's side in working for higher education.' The Liberals were not, in his opinion, up to the mark. Even so, Lord Oxford wrote of his speech on the London University Bill of 1898: 'It is the best thing of the kind I have ever heard in the House of Commons.'

Once again we find that continuity of interest and enthusiasm which always characterized him. On Christmas Eve 1923 he wrote to Ramsay MacDonald: 'Then there is education. On this I have been concentrated for years past and there are definite reforms coming into sight without which my life work would be thrown away.' This was at a time when adult education commanded his energies, such as remained after the faithful discharge of his duties as a Lord of Appeal, undertaken as became an ex-Lord Chancellor.

In 1917 he assured me that all his spare time would be devoted to adult education. So massive were his powers of work that 'spare time' with him was greater than 'whole time' with many.

His imagination was stirred by the vast throngs of working men and women who attended, or sought to get admittance to, the course of lectures delivered by Bishop (then Professor) Masterman, on June Saturdays during 1907–8–9 in Westminster Abbey and in the royal gallery of the House of Lords. It was this experience which made him an enthusiastic lifelong supporter of the Workers' Educational Association and led him later to encourage the formation, and to become a living active president, of the British Institute of Adult Education.

It has been my part and lot in life to witness much self-sacrificing devotion to adult education, but I can say confidently that I have never known any one, man or woman, workman or scholar, who, regardless of trouble, was so ready and instant in doing anything asked of him: whether it were to travel all night to address a group of people, or to gather people round his own hospitable board for the purpose of planning or discussion.

He was the 'adult educationist' of his time. His work in the movement lifted it on to a high level and secured for it widespread attention, not only in England and Wales, but in Scotland and overseas. He only restricted his efforts when increasing weakness brought upon him the prohibition of his doctors.

VI

Nothing became Lord Haldane more than his calm, stoical departure from the scenes of his active life in England. The two last public addresses he delivered were to the Association of Headmistresses on 9th June 1928, and to the working men and women of Swindon, at Upham, on 16th June 1928. To the former he spoke on the 'Relativity of Knowledge.' They tell me he was so gentle and kindly, full of happiness. His concluding words were:

I am sure of this, that if there is any one study which more than any other repays, it is the study of ultimate reality and the attempt to get the grasp which the history of thought gives you of the meaning of these deeper things. There may be no ultimate system of philosophy or metaphysics. I do not think there is, any more than there is anything ultimate possibly even in religion; but at least you can get a grasp of what the whole thing means, which will lead you out of a sea of mental troubles and open up to you an enriched view of the universe.

The address at Upham must have been almost a last testament. He knew the Swindon people well. Over a long period he had not failed to visit them at least once yearly. A workman who was present has just written me, from memory, his account of it. I give it in his own words:

His appeal was, get acquainted with St. John's Gospel. No writer was better acquainted with or knew the lives of the people more than St. John. They would find, especially the women, that he knew them in their homes and in their difficulties. The appeal for tolerance and the endeavour to understand others was there. He, John, showed them how their love should be given to the poor and outcast. He bid them to be happy but above all to try to serve others. . . . In sorrow, in failure, in hope, and in success there lay revealed the life of true womanhood. . . . Such teachings would show them their place and opportunities.

They should also read the trial and death of Socrates.

He showed the part that Socrates played—his noble and brave life—his determination, at all costs, to help others to know the truth. How with grandeur he stood before his accusers with a bearing that won even the admiration of his enemies. As they read they would realize the life and ideals of one of the world's greatest philosophers and teachers. After the address [writes the workman] I walked with him a little. He spoke of the position of the weekly wage earner, and said with warmth and emphasis: 'If they would only aim for spiritual ideals—trade unionists and co-operators—nothing could prevent their rapid progress—they would sweep the field.'

The picture of this simple scene, the last public one of his life, working men and women clustering around him, Lord Haldane invoking the teaching of Socrates and St. John, is one to dwell upon.

It was, as a conclusion to his life, not unlike the text he so often used at the end of his speeches: 'Not every one that saith unto me Lord, Lord, shall enter the kingdom of heaven, but he that doeth the will of my Father which is in heaven.'

He returned to London.

Whatever happened he felt he could not fail to honour the work of his old friend, Randall Thomas Davidson, Archbishop of Canterbury. So, in the afternoon of his last complete day in town, scarcely able to walk, finding it difficult to speak, he attended a meeting of the Testimonial Committee in the Jerusalem Chamber, made his contribution, and his human form passed out of the sight of our eyes for ever. I, at least, felt that I should not see him again. Such an action was in keeping with his life—faithful, strong, sympathetic, generous.

His sister, and those nearest to him, hoped that rest at Cloan might relieve his physical weakness, but it was not to be. Death in those days, as ever, had no fears for him. 'He talked of it as naturally as one might talk of casting off a garment.'

We may leave all that is mortal of him at Gleneagles, the Trinity of his teaching — the Unity of the life dedicated — work, tolerance, love — pulsing through our hearts and minds.

If he were right, however, and he *was* right, Richard Burdon, Viscount Haldane, lives on in that communion beyond the perceptions of the mortal senses of the ordinary men and women he loved and served so well, and, we may trust, still loves and serves: his spirit, inseparable from the infinite, one with God—the dedication of his life accepted.

> And there's another country, I've heard of long ago—
> Most dear to them that love her, most great to them that know—
> We may not count her armies; we may not see her King,
> Her fortress is a faithful heart, her pride is suffering—
> And soul by soul and silently her shining bounds increase.[1]

[1] Cecil Spring Rice.

15. THE DYNAMIC OF LIFE

(The thirty-second Lecture Conference of Works Directors, Managers, Foremen, and Forewomen was held at University College, Oxford, from 29th September to 2nd October 1932; this lecture concluded the proceedings. After a brief summing up of some of the findings of the conference, a résumé is given of some of the lecturer's business experiences, and mention is made of a number of great figures whom he has met. The spiritual power in man, right judgment, and worship as the highest form of love are also considered.)

I AM very happy indeed to be here to-night. I cannot presume to sum up. The chairman politely informed you that I had no business experience—I will tell him in a minute whether I have or not! But I would not claim for myself the capacity to sum up what you have been hearing these last few days. Extraordinarily good it has all been, and extraordinarily high the level of the conference! I noticed that the young men were very quiet. This might, or might not, be due to their humility, but, almost exclusively, the questions and the contributions, some of them of explosive quality, have been made by the older men. I thought this was extremely refreshing.

Very rarely in a conference do we get what people really think. We usually get what people think that other people would like them to think. But this conference has been breaking through that kind of instinctive camouflage, expressing genuine convictions, and one extremely interesting feature of it was that never once were the big principles left without witness. Over and over it was as though a speaker had spread unsuspected wings, and left the floor of so-called realism for the upper air of idealism. It was delightful to note how these excursions were welcomed, and I agree with the chairman that all the while there has been running through this conference a sense of what used to be called 'the great realities'—the big things of life, the things that perhaps we hardly could discuss even if we would. We might touch upon them vaguely, and possibly imagine that we were probing the depths, but we should only be stirring the face of the waters.

The addresses have been directed to increased efficiency, but what has always emerged as the thing to be desired is the human bond between employer and employed. It was underlined by a speech which emphasized the fact that working girls might be 'ladies' just as much as those who happened to be in authority over them. The consciousness of interdependence and co-operation, on both sides, was considered to be fundamental.

One who might have been expected to deal almost entirely with the human body reminded us that the strong emotional reserves of the workers must always be taken into account. We were urged to treat men, not according to their deserts, but according to our own honour and dignity. And in the first address given it seemed to me that the high-water mark was reached, and that we were clearly shown how conventional obligations were transcended by the injunction 'to do justice, and to love mercy, and to walk humbly with thy God.'

I noticed that Mr. Rowntree, speaking in 1927, said:

Unless a country keeps the flames of its spiritual life burning both in industry and politics, sooner or later that country is doomed. Ignore the spiritual life of the nation, and what is left? Only selfish material ends, which separate men from God and one another and which, whether fulfilled or thwarted, lead to loneliness and despair.

Now, I wondered what I was going to call my address to-night. I have been once or twice to the United States, and I remember being asked what I would lecture on. I said: 'Here is a list of twelve titles. Choose which you like, you will get the same lecture!' But whilst the doctor was talking to us about physical health in the factory I got a brain-wave, and I said to myself: 'I will call my address on Sunday night "The Dynamic of Life."' Then I knew that I had got a good title, whatever else followed, because those mere words make one feel more self-reliant and energetic and ready to 'face the foeman in the gate.'

First of all, however, it is up to me to prove that I am a business man. Nobody believes it, but I have a perfectly genuine business record; and when I came down here on Thursday I broke away from a directors' business meeting.

I will not go on to assure you that my fellow directors were sorry to lose me, for I imagine that some of them were relieved. But that is not the point; the point is that I was there!

I began life in business at the age of fourteen. I earned seven shillings and sixpence a week as what was euphemistically called a junior clerk. In reality I was just an office boy, and I dispatched cod-liver oil and guano. I had to go down into the East End of London and send it myself, and I knew what it looked like and what it smelt like!

I was ambitious, and for a little while I got into the junior ranks of the civil service, where you would not, in those days, have expected to find business. In fact, one day, the chief, coming in at an awkward moment, discovered me playing cricket with a soft ball and a stick! 'There is nothing to be done without work,' as the government office clerk said as he cracked a Brazil nut! I ventured next into a retail business, where I was a ledger clerk. Then I went into tea—and the amount of tea I dispatched to the wrong destinations! I remember that once two chests of tea were ordered. But, at the time, I had a flair for salesmanship, and I measured the possible market, and instead of sending two chests I sent two hundred. The man went down with a wheelbarrow and found a train load! No wonder I shiver a little now at the recollection.

I decided to make another shift, and I went into finance. Then it occurred to me that education was my job, and I told people this, and they believed it. So I left business for a while, but went back to the same firm a few years later as a director. As a matter of fact, except for a few years, I have earned my living in business all my life.

I have been thinking that before I get to the dynamic of life, if ever I get there, I would tell you some of the simple, obvious things I have learned in business. I was once much intrigued by a book which was very widely read: *The Letters of a Self-made Merchant to his Son*. It seemed to me to contain a great deal of good and shrewd advice, and I learned much from it. But I learned more in my own business experience, because life was rather rough. There was no question as to the humble nature of my work. I went with high pride to one place, thinking that I was going to be someone of importance, and they put me down to mere messenger boy's work, and I had to be quick at that. And I want to tell you that it is the wisest thing in the world to accept the meanest work without grumbling, if it is given to you by lawful authority. But do you know that when I have to engage clerks (I have been more or less responsible for six offices) I test them out as to what they would be willing to do if they entered my employment? I sometimes suggest the most absurd things, that I should never ask them to do in the normal routine; and if they say they are ready to do them, with a cheerfulness that I can tell is not assumed for the occasion, I feel that they have passed one crucial test. I am not going to tell you the possibilities I have suggested, but you can see the principle.

I used to get 'fed up' with monotonous work, such as adding up figures. I could add them up correctly when I was thinking of something else. We had no adding machines then, but it was pretty clear to me, at all events, that I had no right to protest against a job, or be impatient with it, until I could do it perfectly. And as I never arrived at the stage of perfection there was never a chance of protesting!

Another thing I learned was that business executives, or whatever you call them in modern jargon, the 'bosses,' or the foremen, are short-sighted and stupid if they try to keep everything in their own hands. In these days, perhaps no one *is* so short-sighted and stupid, but they sometimes were in my day. The man who got the job would try to keep his grip of it so completely that if he was away for a fortnight's holiday others would see how much he was missed. But the really successful business man is the man who can be absent and yet his work goes on. That is the test I would apply, and I mean it in absolute seriousness. If the work goes on worse when a man is away, in my eyes he is condemned. The man who feels he must be always on the job, and doing everything himself, and looking round every corner, will never get anywhere, unless somebody else gets him there. Moreover, his suspicious attitude poisons the whole atmosphere. Trust everybody! You get much more out of any group if you trust them. Don't trust them merely to carry out orders, but believe that they have ability, and that the more responsibility devolves on them the better it is for the whole enterprise. Confidence in them develops their self-respect, and enables you to get the advantage of their brains. Any head of a business who is worth his salt should be able, if he has blundered, to accept correction from the office boy; and the boy should feel free to give it, without any suggestion of impertinence. The man who dictates letters must have someone who can put his commas right, and put his grammar right, and even say the thing better than he has said it, if possible! If I had a secretary, and she answered: 'But you said it,' when I told her something was wrong, I would say: 'Well, it's your business, if I say the wrong thing, to put it right!' That kind of reliance on others makes them far more competent and reliable.

One other obvious thing. There is no man living who is capable of doing a complicated job by himself. He has not got the necessary qualities. The longer I live the more convinced I am that we supplement one another. As Ecclesiasticus has said: 'Do nothing without advice; and when thou hast once done, repent not.'[1] I have seen men in high positions who consider themselves quite capable of supplying every quality that is essential to an enterprise, and they select staffs whose members are all alike, like peas in a pod. But that is a foolish thing to do! The fact is that they themselves have not the perception to realize that many types and many qualities are needed if the enterprise is to be a rich and complete whole. However excellent flutes may be you can't play a symphony with flutes alone, and it is the same with industry. We must blend elements that at first might seem incongruous, if we are to achieve full and rich industrial harmony.

Business teaches one to think those things out. Another thing I learned in my chequered experience was that it is possible to be honest in business. I don't say that the path

[1] Ecclesiasticus, xxxii. 19.

of complete and utter frankness is always open to every employer, however high his ideals. But, fortunately, I have been connected for forty-seven years with a business which I have never known, in the whole of that period, to be guilty of deliberate misrepresentation or meanness. And, of course, there is a still larger honesty. At one time in my life I used to buy the products of a certain firm because its standard of integrity was so high that in doing so I felt that I was benefiting the whole community. I know, however, that honesty in business is a difficult thing. Jesus the son of Sirach wrote in Ecclesiasticus about two hundred years before the coming of Christ: 'As a nail sticketh fast between the joining of the stone, so doth sin stick close between buying and selling.' [1]

He also spoke caustically of people whose first desire is to get rich. His comment was:

Watching for riches consumeth the flesh, and the care thereof driveth away sleep. . . . He that loveth gold shall not be justified, and he that followeth corruption shall have enough thereof. Gold hath been the ruin of many, and their destruction was present. [2]

But to come back to my business life, and what it has taught me. It has taught me this about employees. The more awkward the youngster is, the more chance is there that he will turn out to be a successful man. Somehow, the individual who is always there, always to time, with a clean collar and everything nice, remains there for the rest of his life. The two most awkward little demons—perfect terrors—that I ever worked with have proved to be the most successful men in the highest reaches of business. But they simply worried the life out of me!

I must refer to one very successful business man who seemed to have retained the heart of a little child, and who strove with all his might to help others. He himself had had no opportunity of becoming a scholar. Therefore he made as many opportunities as possible for young men and young women to get scholarships and further their education, and he did countless other things to benefit the community. But he helped me to realize that it is true, in business as everywhere

---

[1] Ecclesiasticus, xxvii. 2.   [2] Ecclesiasticus, xxx. 1, 5, 6.

else, that 'except a man become as a little child, he shall in no wise enter the kingdom of heaven.' Some of you may have guessed that I mean Thomas Wall. But nothing I can say will give you the least idea of that man's beautiful and true spirit; and he asked no thanks, no more thanks than I should expect if I surreptitiously put a halfpenny into the collecting bag on a Sunday. His was just the joy of the giver, who feels that he is thanked or rewarded because people consent to receive from him.

I want to pay a tribute to two people outside the business world, because they have taught me so much.

I think my great teacher was Charles Gore, who died last year. He faced this question of justice and honour and truth in business with a single heart; and he did a great deal, far more than people know, to help to bring about better relations in industry. The first time I had any definite concrete action with him was when, in a certain London stores, which shall be nameless, there was manifest injustice. He promised me nothing; but he set to work quietly, and he became a shareholder and went to an annual meeting, and lifted his voice. It was a voice crying in the wilderness, but it was strong, and it had effect.

In another industrial dispute, after long and difficult investigation, he assured himself as to the rights and wrongs of the case. It was in a factory, and he stood by the men with whom he sympathized. He did this not only in virtue of his position as Bishop of Oxford, but actually in the board room with the directors. The matter involved a firm which shall be nameless now; but when I knew it there was a wail of agony going up from the workpeople. To-day, however, its reputation stands high.

Then there was Margaret McMillan—I think perhaps the most wonderful person of her time. I cannot give you her biography to-night, but she was one who listened to the voice of the Spirit, and having heard it went out, and did not trouble as to what was in front of her. The result is that there is not a child in any of the elementary schools of this country but has a chance of better health because of her. As Charles Gore

G

himself said, in a little book paying tribute to her that was published after his death, it shows what tremendous results can come from the devotion of one simple life, which had no worldly advantages, but which was guided by the voice of the Spirit.

And now I must drop these reminiscences.

Here we are—in a chaotic world; at all events the surface of the world seems unusually chaotic, even if underneath it is the same old world! And there are so many clanging voices. To-day I cannot bear to buy a Sunday newspaper, even of the better sort, because of the clanging voices within it. I have bought Sunday newspapers for the last twenty years, but I am coming to the conclusion, as I grow older, that it may be better to leave them alone, and get back to some books that are worth while. You may say that I shall be behind the times. But the fact is that I shall not! If you want a right judgment on human affairs, don't try to sift out the truth from the latest contradictory opinions of even first-class journalism, but go to the great old thinkers, and you will find your judgment almost insensibly clarified. I am not speaking, of course, of specific items of definite information; but in these days, what with wireless and other amenities, there is precious little chance of missing them, even if you never open a newspaper.

I do not for a moment believe that 'the days are evil.' In 1926, on this platform, I said: 'Now, there is a good deal of talk about the decay of humanity, of institutions, and of nations. Some say that England is played out, others that western civilization is at its last lap. What will happen we do not know; but we do know that if we look at things in the right way, and strive to order the material of the world aright, there will be no such decay as is prophesied.'

I am always strengthened by the thought that never in the history of any nation has there been so clearly manifest the influence of the teaching and life of Jesus Christ as in the English community to-day. It may be largely because there were people, fifty years ago, who set on foot most of the movements that have brought about this result; and it may emphasize our own responsibility for making sacrifices now on behalf of the generations yet unborn.

Look at some of the changes. If any one is out of work to-day, will he starve? No workman need starve, although he may have only the barest livelihood. If there was a strike, people used to say: 'Let them starve. They will soon come to their senses.' But nobody dare say that now, and we have tried, in our blundering way, to secure to every man, woman, or child the sheer necessaries of life. Doubtless, we might have done better—but assuredly we might have done worse.

Another thing I have noticed. How nice people are to one another! Look at the kindness shown in the streets! My experience is that the huge majority of people are more eager to help one another than they used to be. There is a kind of good-natured comradeship amongst the English people, and it is going to help to save us from the trouble that otherwise might have fallen on this nation.

The English workman bears no personal grudge whatever against the man who is rich. I have taken Socialists and Communists down into country houses, and they have been charmed beyond words. It has not altered their economic outlook, but they have seen that human beings, rich or poor, are much alike. And this kind of tolerant comprehension of the other man's difficulties and limitations will be an important factor in the avoidance of serious conflict.

Now, you may be saying inwardly: 'But where do we come in?' Well, each of us is an individual. Some people will tell you that we are only dust, which gradually raises itself, or is raised by a curious process called evolution, into wonderful and complex organisms which we speak of as humanity, and which then degenerates into lower forms of life. This view has a certain vogue among people who are clever enough to hide themselves from themselves. Its adherents are generally very clever and very stupid; but they are not altogether to blame. They would blunder less if the people who hold very different views really believed the views they held.

A human being is a trinity of body, mind, and spirit. We know that it would be impossible, on this plane, to express ourselves without our bodies; we know, too, the terrible pathos of a body that is tenanted by a disordered mind, and realize the blessings of sanity. But comparatively few people seem to think that the element of the spirit is equally necessary. I say 'equally' because in this life all three are necessary, but I don't want to put one above the other, but I am positive that more troubles are caused in this world by people who try to ignore and suppress the facts of the spiritual life than by people whose minds or bodies are completely out of gear.

I happened to pick up a book on *Materialism* by Professor J. S. Haldane, and he says quite definitely that 'if we lose sight of the spiritual world we lose sight of what alone is ultimately real in ourselves,' and we fail to realize ourselves. 'Spiritual reality is the only reality.' Professor J. S. Haldane belongs to no church. He is an eminent scientist in this university, and he is only re-echoing what, as you know, Lord Haldane was always saying. Lord Haldane, in his later years, continually stressed one thing—'that the spiritual alone is real.' I might add a further quotation from Professor J. S. Haldane:

Men very commonly accept in practice the metaphor of the machine, taking this metaphor for a complete representation of industrial reality; and it seems to me that wholly unnatural instability in the relations between employers and employed is the result. I am convinced that the real driving force behind what is called labour unrest is just human rebellion against what are regarded as inhuman relations.

This contention was based, of course, upon the writer's spiritual view of life.

To sum it up—we have got to do our work in the world, and the spiritual life within us is the only thing which is eternal and undying. Our bodies pass; the brains through which our minds function turn to dust; but something remains; you may call it your soul or your spirit, or you may call it a ray, an emanation from the eternal mind that itself is but one aspect of the universal consciousness.

But if spirit is the only real thing, the one object of our lives in the world is to become channels for the expression of spiritual forces. We have no other purpose on this earth, and we create the spirit's channels by every right thought that we think. I am less concerned with speech and action.

I believe that the real power in human life is the thought, whether it be expressed or not. Can you remember that? Of course, I cannot prove it. I am not going to try to prove it. But I am quite certain that if any one fully believes that his thinking moulds his own life, and very profoundly affects the lives of those around him, and reacts on the whole universe, and thinks in accordance with that belief—all other things will be added unto him. The actions and habits of men must be preceded by the thoughts of men. Turn to what Plato said long ago:

> He therefore who hath always been occupied with the cravings of desire and ambition, and who busieth himself wholly therewith, will of necessity have got all his notions mortal, and as far as possible he will become altogether mortal. But he who hath earnestly striven after learning and true wisdom, and hath been fully trained and exercised therein, he, if he lay hold on truth, must, one would think of necessity, acquire an immortal and heavenly temper.

So we come to the idea that our business is to live at our own best, and not at somebody else's best. Dynamic power is the power of the spirit to get the best out of us.

Again, Shakespeare said in *Hamlet*:

> Sure, he that made us with such large discourse,
> Looking before and after gave us not
> That capability and godlike reason
> To fust in us unused.

'Fust,' incidentally, is a splendid word, but think for a moment of Shakespeare's message to us all in the lines just quoted.

Every man in this room is more wonderful than he has ever dreamed himself. But we are so accustomed to the amazing wonder of our being that we forget it. We become enmeshed in our puny schemes and our puny desires, till we create for ourselves a kind of false isolation which we call reality.

And all the while we can only be 'real' as part of a great pattern that both transcends and completes our lives—some universal plan which we can only find peace in serving to the best of our power. And if any of you thinks that he has no chance to serve that plan he is utterly mistaken. We can serve it in wealth or poverty, in health or sickness; we can serve it whether we are brilliant or stupid—only one thing is essential, and that is to forget ourselves, and surrender thought and will to the guidance of a greater Will and a greater Thought.

Sometimes it is as if St. Paul had covered all the ground that I am trying to cover, in the thirteenth of Corinthians, in his words about charity. For charity, or love, means leaving behind all selfish isolation, and entering into a vaster life. It means that we are all members of one body, and that no one can suffer, no one can fail, alone. It means the sense of unity, and of willing sacrifice for the whole of which we are a part, that is the mother of all the virtues, and greater than them all. That sense of unity is a very beautiful and a very joyful thing, if only because it casts out jealousy, which is one of the saddest things in the world. Jealousy may or may not hurt the person towards whom it is directed, but it always hurts terribly the person who feels it. And it can only be banished by this knowledge that every worthy or beautiful thing belonging to another, or done by another, is mine, made mine by my own reverence, and admiration, and love. A lovely song enriches not only the singer, but all who recognize its loveliness, and its influence is broadcast far and wide by a kind of living wireless.

Love will teach us all things [said Dostoevsky in *The Brothers Karamazov*], but we must learn how to win love; it is got with difficulty; it is a possession dearly bought with much labour and in long time; for one must love not sometimes only, for a passing moment, but always. There is no man who doth not sometimes love; even the wicked can do that. And let not men's sin dishearten thee; love a man even in his sin, for that love is a likeness of the divine love, and is the summit of love on earth. Love all God's creation, both the whole and every grain of sand.

If thou lovest each thing thou wilt perceive the mystery of God in all; and when once thou perceivest this, thou wilt thenceforward grow every day to a fuller understanding of it; until thou comest to love the whole world with a love that will then be all-embracing and universal.

'To love man in his sin!' I will not expand that—but think of it! And so love comes out in integrity and sincerity, in home, in business, in life, in the world. It gives us our vision of world unity—the vision that came to John when he wrote of the Holy City: 'And the kings of the earth do bring their glory and honour into it.' Every nation will bring its treasures, its experience, its outstanding capacities—all that it knows of beauty and of goodness, to enrich the one great harmony. John wrote also, of course, that there would enter into that city 'nothing that defileth or maketh a lie.' But that surely only means that sin and falsehood fall away from poor faulty human beings as they draw near the city's gate.

Love, then, is the dynamic of life. We gain strength from it, not because we say we are going to gain strength from it, but because it lifts us out of the weakness, the captivity, of selfishness. It is of the spirit; and those who live in the spirit become, as it were, power-houses, both receiving and giving out all that is best and truest. That is true greatness.

In deep humility men must search the inmost depths of their hearts, seeking their 'I believe'; and having found it, they must nourish and tend it, by all that is most true and beautiful in the range of their perceptions, that it may grow and expand, and transfigure all the relations of their lives. The man who has no 'I believe' is unstable in all his ways. He seeks furtively, nervously, and stealthily to snatch at the fancied advantages of this life—mistaking shadows for substance—and useless trash for treasure of infinite worth.

Strong was he that had a Church [said Carlyle]. What we can call a Church; he stood thereby, though in the centre of Immensitudes, in the conflux of Eternities. Yet manlike towards God and man; the vague shoreless Universe had become a firm city for him, a dwelling which he knew. Such virtue was in Belief; in the words well-spoken 'I believe.' But of those decadent ages in which no ideal either grows or blossoms; when Belief and Loyalty have passed away, and only the cant and false echo of them remains; and all Solemnity has become Pageantry; and the creed of persons in authority—an Imbecility or a Machiavelism? Alas, of these ages world history can take no notice—blotted out as spurious—which indeed they are. Hapless ages, wherein, if ever in any, it is an unhappiness to be born. To be born and to learn only, by every tradition and example that God's Universe is Belial and a Lie; and the supreme Quack the monarch of men. In which mournfullest faith, nevertheless, do we not see whole generations—live what they call living and vanish.

In other words, worship is the highest form of love, and only from the standpoint which sincere worship gives can a man see his real self, and what he is meant to be.   That is the way of all true advance.

But worship gives men and women courage.

> Bring me my Bow of burning gold!
>   Bring me my Arrows of desire!
> Bring me my Spear!   O clouds unfold!
>   Bring me my Chariot of fire!
>
> I will not cease from mental fight,
>   Nor shall my sword sleep in my hand,
> Till we have built Jerusalem
>   In England's green and pleasant land!

16. THE DEMANDS OF THE ORDINARY MAN

(This article was written for a volume edited by Dr. Percy Dearmer, called *Christianity and the Crisis*, published in 1933. The aim of the book was to suggest the relationship of Christianity to the everyday life of man, especially as regards present-day problems. That the ordinary man forms the vast bulk of humanity is the chief thesis; the world crisis is defined, and its main causes (mechanization and urbanization) are discussed. The effects of Christianity on English life are considered at some length, and the demand on the ordinary man is shown to be an increase in his efforts to make actual the wisdom and love derived from God.)

JUST as the body of the individual contains parts or organs, created or evolved for special purposes, which, functioning rightly, minister to the good of the whole, so it is certain that humanity, whether it be regarded as one body or not, is served by men who are endowed with diverse gifts, even though they live and move in the same environment. The bulk of men are ordinary. This does not mean that they are inferior, but simply that they have no recognizable special gifts. They are as important in the scheme of things as the limbs of the body of man are in relation to his eyes, ears, nerves, and brain. If they are not healthy in body, mind, and spirit, the extraordinary men—those, roughly speaking, of ascertainable special ability—are handicapped in their functioning. 'God must have loved ordinary people; He made so many of them.'

To-day, the ordinary man is beset on all sides, particularly by those who expect him to have clearly thought-out ideas, not on one main subject only, but on all.

Whether it is agreeable or not, there can be no doubt that only a small percentage—not more than twenty per cent under the best conditions—have the power to think on matters, abstract or concrete, which do not come within the range of their everyday experience.

Yet all are urged to do so, and knowledge is flung before their eyes and in their ears. They are inevitably confused. If they were not impervious they would be ruined.

All men respond, consciously or unconsciously, to the

forces which operate in their natural life. They also respond in greater or less degree to the motions of their spirit. The big things in life come unsought to men.

The important thing is not that they shall understand with their minds, but that they shall live their life to the full, and that, so living, they shall do their work in the world, whether it be mental or manual, writing books or ploughing fields, and do it all in healthy relationship with their fellows. But such a healthy relationship is only created as the inevitable outcome of love and worship, the primary instincts of normal men.

It is essential, therefore, that a consideration of Christianity in relation to a state of affairs in England and in the world so acute as to justify the term 'crisis' should be preceded by an attempt to express the demands of the non-specialist ordinary man. He represents the vast bulk of humanity. His point of view is necessarily of immense importance, for it at once affects, and is affected by, the researches and efforts of those experts—theologians, philosophers, historians, or economists —who have set forth their own specific analysis of the nature of the problems and their own approach to solutions.

It may be urged that ordinary men who are not Christians have no right to make demands; but this can only possibly carry weight if it is confined to the content of faith. All men are potentially Christians, and they are justified in demanding that Christians shall so think and act as to bear compelling witness.

There is a world hunger for all that Christianity claims to give, as a tree gives its fruits.

Thus from the point of view of the ordinary man the position and place of Christianity in its relationship to the crisis may be examined, and reasonable demands made upon those who proclaim 'that the application of Christian principles is the way by which the world can recover and move forward.'

1. The Crisis Defined

'Civilization is at the cross-roads.' If this recurrent platitude has any truth in relation to the present time, it is that
one road, with material and superficial promise, may lead to
decline, and perhaps ruin; the other road, through spiritual
and deep happiness, may lead to increasing health and power.
The title of this volume, *Christianity and the Crisis*, suggests
that there is an eternal and spiritual force to be brought to
bear upon a temporal and material condition.

The feeling of crisis is accentuated by the widespread consciousness of it. The unending reception of bad news tends
to depress even the most optimistic minds. It damps the spirit
of adventure, wears confidence away, and induces mass paralysis.

The evil of it all would be diminished if the sources and
background of life were kept in mind, and if good news were
circulated as readily as bad.

'Who will show us any good? Oh, for a prince in Israel!'

It is easy for us to imagine that there has never been such
a crisis before. 'The hungry forties' is no more than an ugly
phrase. The Napoleonic Wars and their effects are viewed
through the visions of a final dramatic victory and a pros-
perous later Victorian age.

A modern novelist has collected utterances of outstanding
men and women of the last century which show that they too
were burdened with a sense of impending crisis no less heavy
than ours. 'There is scarcely anything round us but ruin
and despair,' said William Pitt. Queen Adelaide had only
one desire—'to play the part of Marie Antoinette with
bravery in the revolution that is coming in England.' Wilberforce dared not marry because the future was so dark and
unsettled. Lord Shaftesbury prophesied that nothing could
save the British Empire from shipwreck. Disraeli thought
that in industry, commerce, and agriculture there was no
hope, and the Duke of Wellington said on the day before he
died: 'I thank God I shall be spared from seeing the con-
summation of ruin that is gathering about us.'

It would seem that the present crisis has been in part

precipitated by man's power to invent instruments and machinery which, because he gives himself up to them, he is unable to control.

The problem is an ancient one. Invention is good in itself. 'I, wisdom, dwell with prudence and find out know-ledge of witty inventions.'[1] But when inventions get out of their proper place in the life of man, then only are they to be deplored. 'Lo, this only have I found, that God hath made man upright; but they have sought out many inventions.'[2] The result is inevitable. 'Thus they provoked him to anger with their inventions: and the plague brake in upon them.'[3] The Old Testament writers had different inventions in mind. 'They made a calf in Horeb and worshipped the molten image.'[4] To-day the images are different but the golden calf still stands on its ancient pedestal. As a result the crisis breaks in upon us.

Man has largely solved the problems of mass production, but has made no corresponding advance in the problems of mass distribution. The trouble goes deeper. The nature of man demands that he shall occupy himself in healthy toil which has a reasonable objective. By so doing he keeps his body right and his mind awake. He generates power. High mental and spiritual enterprise depends for its strength and inspiration upon the right living of all men. But mechan-ization and urbanization force too many men from the work they would do in the place they would occupy.

The dilemma is real, yet it ought to be resolved. 'Wisdom should dwell with prudence' and 'witty inventions' should minister to the development and sustenance of healthy human beings. Our day is being tested and tried, and the incidence of judgment will rest upon the kind of men and women we are, not upon the piles of elegant and inelegant material we have collected.

Nothing less than strenuous effort on the part of individuals and nations who recognize the unity of all men will enable man to manage his material. Wisdom and not cleverness will serve men best.

[1] Proverbs viii. 12.   [2] Ecclesiastes, vii. 29.   [3] Psalm cvi. 29.   [4] Psalm cvi. 19.

There are now, as always, certain types of clever people, relying unduly upon their own brains, and out of touch with reality, who say that 'Life is short and tedious'; 'We are born at all adventure'; 'Let us enjoy the good things that are present'; 'Let none of us go without his part of our voluptuousness.'[1]

They accentuate the 'crisis' while they help it to continue. Happily, their influence will spend itself, since they deal with superficial things. The realities remain in their deeps untroubled. Yet such men can spoil human life, both in individuals and nations, even to the destruction of health and happiness.

If an increasing number of men will think of the good of all men and forget their 'voluptuousness,' the channels of just and equitable distribution now blocked by the masses of production will be gradually freed, and a growth of confidence among men will dismiss the 'crisis' with rapidity.

Meanwhile much encouragement may be derived from the effect of Christian action already on English life. In spite of the glaring defects of maldistribution, social life and relationships are more in harmony with the highest and best interests of man than they have ever been in the centuries of recorded history. It is not merely developed humanitarianism but the ethic of Christ, translated into the terms of the community by men avowedly working in the power of the Holy Spirit. This ethic and this power have been kept, in word and teaching at least, consistently before men by the Churches.

Great and outstanding reforms have almost without exception been initiated by Christians. This present year is the centenary of the abolition of slavery in the British Empire and of the chief Factory Act. Wilberforce and Shaftesbury were inspired by their faith in Christ. The Churches also were the begetters and the nursing mothers of education, not only in universities, but in the nineteenth-century rise of schools for the children of the poor.

It is beside the point to deplore that Christians, in the face of great need, with the vision of the City of God on earth before their eyes, were slack and slow, much too concerned with their

[1] Wisdom of Solomon, ii. 1, 2, 6, 9.

own comfortable lives. They did move; and their force was irresistible; the facts are clear.

No one can imagine what the present state of the English community would be if Christianity had never found foothold in Britain. Ghastly things have been done in its name, but it is certain that no higher or better force has ever entered or been expressed in the whole story of English life. Every ethic that is worth while either derives from it or is in harmony with it. But the English community is not what it should be, and could be, if an increasing number of sincere Christians trained themselves for service in its behalf.

II. The Place of Christianity in English Life

Corporate bodies of Christians united in great churches are so numerous and powerful as to justify great demands being made on them. The Churches are certain that by the grace of God they are wells of living water in a thirsty land, Those who drink go out refreshed, courageous, devoted, loving, to face and deal with the problems of daily life in the community.

Looked at from any point of view the Churches are the most widespread institutions in the national life. They have been, and still are, the most powerful. The population of England and Wales was nearly forty millions in 1931, of whom about sixteen millions were children or adolescents. At least seven million adults are duly enrolled members of Churches. The electoral rolls of the Church of England contain three and a half million names, and vast numbers besides have never claimed the franchise. In the country villages, for example, they are shy of signing papers. There are certainly not less than two million adult members of Nonconformist bodies, and roughly one and a half million adults in the Roman communion. These figures are sufficient to reveal that there is a real heart of Christian belief in England.

After all allowance has been made for those who regard Christian worship as little more than a respectable and desirable amenity, it is clear and certain that Christianity is in a position to exercise a powerful influence on human affairs and relations, whether individual, national, or international. Apart from the membership of the Churches, it may be confidently asserted that the temper of ordinary men is at bottom religious. There is no court of appeal more readily admitted than the teachings of Jesus. At critical moments the majority of men turn to religion for sanction or consolation.

Older men have seen positive atheism become negligible, either replaced by reverent agnosticism or sometimes by belief. At the same time family prayers in workshop or home have almost died out, while the family Bible is regarded almost entirely as an heirloom. Sunday observance is now not insisted upon, except in limited circles or in special areas. But co-operators and trade unionists are always ready to attend special services arranged for them. Books dealing with religious subjects are often good sellers, and sometimes best sellers. There is an increasing demand for classes in religious subjects, and would be more if it were not for the retarding influence of sectarian difficulties. Such difficulties are steadily diminishing in schools owing to concordats between the Churches.

On the other side is a group of 'intellectuals' who combine an attitude of contemptuous, or at best indifferent, scepticism towards the Christian faith with a determined attack on the Christian moral standard. They make a strong appeal to many young men and women in universities who are not rooted and grounded in the Faith. For the rest, apart from the widespread reverent agnosticism that is expressed by those who realize the place of spiritual force in human life, the bulk of people more or less outside the Churches are where they are because of preoccupation with the affairs of this world, a preoccupation forced upon some by poverty and others by riches. 'Give me neither poverty nor riches.'

III. The Development of the Ordinary Man and his Demand

At present the sound of many voices is heard in the land, and it is difficult for any one of them not to be lost in the welter of noise. In many ways the experts cancel one another out. Those who have no special knowledge listen in bewilderment. The ordinary man's demand is not 'Give us more knowledge,' but 'Give us a good will and heart to use knowledge and material aright.'   It is misuse that has made our chaos.

The ordinary man is the product of the working of many forces.   He is in part the creature of his environment, which nowadays may be said to include the whole world.   Yet his thought is English, not perhaps in its content, but in its method and quality.   His forerunners stood firm on this island, and absorbed the qualities of diverse races, both conquerors and conquered.   In the English land they evolved the English character, compounded of the characteristics that were in many nations.   The climate and the position helped; but that character had for its dynamic force the motion and rhythm of Christianity.   It is impossible for ordinary men to ignore this force either in their lives or work.   In untroubled days they may forget it for a time; but it is in their make-up, and one day or another it will assert itself.   The ordinary man is potentially, even when not actually, religious.

By the power of the Spirit Christianity entered the lives of his forbears, expressed and revealed to them by the missionaries of Christ.   It gradually became the dominant fact in the land.   When the Romans left it in A.D. 443, 'The Christian missionaries,' writes G. M. Trevelyan, 'alone among the emissaries of civilization did not desert the Britons in their day of trouble.'   The hordes of the Northmen poured into the land; they came in allegiance to Odin, and they grew into that of Christ.   As the centuries passed Christianity continued to mould English life.   It gave birth to characteristic institutions whilst it covered the land with its churches. Clergy were to be found in the midst of every national happening. They stood always in word and teaching, if not always in deed, for the rights of the poor and oppressed. But the importance of the Church declined in the eyes of men as the institutions it had created increased their power and sought uncontrolled liberty. This is clearly exemplified in the story of the universities of Oxford and Cambridge, and also in the history of Parliament.

During the last century or so the Church has still continued to create institutions for amelioration, education, and reform; but its essential task has been to ensure that all the institutions of modern civilization shall be infused and permeated with the Christian spirit. 'The impetus which drove me first of all into the Labour movement,' wrote Keir Hardie, 'and the inspiration which carried me on in it, has been derived more from the teachings of Jesus of Nazareth than from all other sources combined. Many of the best workers in the movement are men who know their New Testament almost by heart, but,' he adds, 'they have been driven out from the churches by the travesty and burlesque of the gospel which there passes for the truth.'

This 'travesty and burlesque' to which Keir Hardie refers had in his mind no connection with doctrine. It referred to glaring insincerity, to the willingness to oppress employees, and to the worship of material position in those who at the same time uttered the high things of God. To him 'the Kingdom of God meant the establishment right here upon earth of a condition of things in which human life would be free to develop on Godlike lines.' He voiced the demand on Christians of all clear-sighted, ordinary men as they make it in time of crisis. The general demand may be analysed in many ways, but in the main it is for sincerity and radiance. It is not concerned with doctrine, but with true and right living, based on the example of Christ.

The demand—the challenge to the ministers of Christ—is to strive, and to induce their flocks to strive, for conformity with the spiritual in life, and to place diminishing reliance on material things—on all that is not essential for right living. It is not indeed their function to attempt the solution of

economic and social problems, but it is their duty to inspire
men to approach them in a right way, without ulterior motive,
to combat evil by the insistence on and practice of good, and
in their radiant faith and confidence to welcome all genuine
efforts of thought and discovery.   It is for them to show that
effort on man's part to create things that are pure and lovely
is in reality a part of his worship, and should be accepted and
hallowed by the Church in her work of building the Kingdom
of God.   This is no time for half-heartedness.   'Is not my
word like as a fire? saith the Lord; and like a hammer that
breaketh the rock in pieces?'   A fire that burns all that is
false, a hammer that breaks rocks in the path.   The earth is
designed for the right living of all men, using their bodies and
minds happily and well in the power of the Spirit.   Christians
are challenged to work in the power of their faith to see that
the intentions of God are carried out.

It may be said that this demand is too simple, too plati-
tudinous; but it *is* the demand, and just in so far as it is
answered, so the wisdom from heaven will have way made for
it, and will lead men to the haven where they would be.

For Christianity, in the record of the Gospels, is absolute
actuality incorporated into human life.   It stands revealed
both in the witness of history and in the urge of the present.
The expression of its creative force among men, in the terms
of the righteousness, justice, and love of God, has been effective
or non-effective in so far as Churches and men have yielded
themselves to it.   The mission of the Churches and of individual Christians is, by intensifying their own faithfulness,
to extend the area of the operation of this force of God in the
world.   Wherever and whenever they succeed order will
replace chaos in human life and affairs.

The struggle of Christians to be faithful has never been
without witness.   At a time of crisis the demand is that they
shall increase their efforts to make actual among men that
wisdom and love which they derive from God.   It is theirs to
bring the force of reality to play upon that misdirection of
human effort, and that maldistribution of human necessities,
which have produced the present crisis in human affairs.

17. SOME WORKMAN SCHOLARS

(On 11th March 1937 this foundation oration was delivered in the theatre of the Institute of Education, University of London. The educated man is defined, 'not necessarily a scholar,' and particulars are given concerning the ideals and achievements of several known and unknown workman scholars.)

I AM very happy indeed to come here to-night. It is not an unfamiliar experience to me; I have, I believe, delivered two addresses here. I do not know whether they were described so highly as foundation orations, but there were two. On the whole you look about the same keen and eager people. I imagine it was six or seven o'clock in the evening when I came here on previous years, and I see the same back bench—in fact, tradition apparently insists on this back bench.

Well, I am very happy, as I have said, to come, and I think perhaps that it may be of interest to you to know of some people who have faced incredible, impossible difficulties to get what we are pursuing, education and learning, and I hope that it will cheer you, and that you will regard them, in some sense, as founders of what this place stands for.

Now just a few remarks at the beginning. An educated man—'man' in the sense the parson means when he says 'brethren'—is not necessarily a scholar. He is one who has found out the way, whether consciously or unconsciously, to make the best of his whole being in the power of his spirit. That is my definition of an educated man, and one does not necessarily look for them in universities like Oxford and Cambridge. I hope I may look for them in the Institute of Education. But as a matter of fact, one of the most educated men I have ever known was a simple gardener who exhibited all the characteristics of a fine mind. He loved his flowers, he was cheerful and happy amongst his people, and he could eat well and he could sleep well. I think those last two things are really essential in the educated man. And now, what is the purpose of education? I invented this once and I thought it was so good that I can never give an address on education without quoting it! The purpose of education is in the power of the spirit through knowledge and training to order the material of the world for the welfare of man and the glory of God. I challenge even the staff here to improve on that!

Now you—at least, some of you—are having a first-class opportunity to learn. I always feel when addressing university students that they must overcome the handicap of having opportunity. I sometimes think that the best work is got out of those who have the courage to face and get over handicaps. If they did not have the difficulties they would not get to the top. Opportunity is often a real handicap. Now workman scholars have, in general, had little or no opportunity. I have in my hand a document which was sent to me by Sir Percy Nunn, whose work I shall always hold in reverence. An old bricklayer wrote to him last year telling him about his difficulties, and Sir Percy sent me a copy of his letter. I think you might like to hear the relevant part of it:

A few weeks ago I had the good fortune to get a cheap copy, second-hand, of the *Teaching of Algebra, including Trigonometry,* also the two books of exercises, with answers. (1914)—I have come to a period of life that gives me leisure (age seventy-two years). The last work was helping to build Manchester New Grammar School (bricklayer). I am interested in the study of mathematics, physics, and astronomy, and would like to use my leisure in learning the various subjects that lead up to astronomy. ·

Your *Teaching of Algebra* appeals to me as an extraordinary book for a self-taught student to use.

Would you kindly advise me what text-books and authors to use? I shall begin with arithmetic and geometry, but I do not want Euclids to start with.

Unfortunately, new text-books are expensive, therefore I must get second-hand copies, gradually. My income is small, 10s. old age pension, plus a small weekly charity of 7s. 6d. Thirty-five years back I attended three winter classes:

Workshop arithmetic and mensuration (first-class pass).
Geometrical drawing.
Machine construction, inking in.

All the classes at Manchester municipal technical school. I began work at nine and a half years of age. I was born only half a mile from the castle, in the parish of Gresham, Norfolk, where the noted family of Greshams lived—Sir Thomas G—— (1519?–79), who founded the London Exchange, also Gresham College, where there are free lectures on astronomy, besides other subjects.

Gresham's School, Holt, Norfolk, was also founded by one of his relatives—now governed by the Worshipful Company of Fishmongers.

C. F. Gauss, German, mathematician, astronomer, also Professor Samuel

Vince, of Cambridge University, mathematician, astronomer, in their youth found patrons to rescue them from the bricklaying. I was not so fortunate. Therefore, I am trying to know a little about astronomy, etc., in my age.

This is an example of the workman scholar, and I think, as Sir Percy Nunn doubtless thought, that it was a genuine expression of desire. You may smile at it in some ways, and say: 'How can an old man of seventy-two ever hope to get anywhere?' But do any of you get anywhere? And what does it matter, so long as you really enjoy what you are doing and are using your brains? Those people who decry study on the part of old people I detest utterly.

I knew some aged people between sixty and seventy who got together to study French. I have my doubts as to what would happen when they got to France, but they greatly enjoyed saying 'Comment vous portez-vous?' and so on, to each other.

Now it is not commonly recognized that many of the world's greatest scholars have been manual workers, and as often as not, sons of labouring people. Let me give you some illustrations. George Green, the mathematician, did manual work in a small mill in Nottingham before he went to Cambridge. Samuel Lee, Professor of Arabic at Cambridge, was a carpenter. Porson, Regius Professor of Greek, was the son of a Norfolk hand-weaver. Thomas Okey, Professor of Italian at Cambridge, was a basket-maker and worked sometimes sixteen hours a day in a cellar making baskets. Joseph Wright, Professor of Comparative Philology at Oxford, and editor of the *English Dialect Dictionary*, was a Yorkshire mill-hand, and did not even learn to read until he was sixteen years of age. And as it was suggested that my illustrations ought not to be wholly English, I think of that great scholar, Masaryk, the first president of Czechoslovakia. His father was a coachman, and he himself began work in a blacksmith's shop. Einstein began his discoveries while he was a clerk in the Swiss Patent Office, and Jacob Boehme was a shoemaker. Spinoza composed his *Ethics* while earning a precarious livelihood by polishing optical glasses. Bunyan, the tinker, wrote the *Pilgrim's Progress* while earning a scanty subsistence in jail. (Jails are better now: you get your food—I know!) And so on. You can go on as long as you like.

I once went into the library at Trinity College, Cambridge, and in the flyleaf of an open book there an eighteenth-century scholar had written the authors of great classics and what their fathers were, and they were all workmen. Of course, in the seventeenth and eighteenth centuries poor scholars went to Oxford as servitors and to Cambridge as sizars. When the rich men went to Oxford and Cambridge they had to have someone to do their lessons for them. The bulk of the population of Oxford and Cambridge was poor, and the rich men didn't want to stop there and become fusty old dons—they wanted to get out into the world and make the tour like the rest of the wealthy young men. And so the poor man rose to the top. Bishop Watson, who was the greatest pluralist of his time, so he ought to know, wrote in 1814: 'The most learned and alive men in Cambridge have ever arisen from that order.' But not all poor men in that day benefited. They don't all benefit now. Some of them were tempted to become vain and silly, while some, according to Macklin, 'were unable to stond straight in the presence of a great man, but boowed and boowed as if it were by instinct.' There were indeed many tuft-hunters among them. As for the costs in those days, George Whitefield—being used to drawing beer in his mother's beer shop in Gloucester and quick in opening bottles—got his Oxford education at Pembroke College at a total cost to his relatives of £24 for three years. But Samuel Wesley, the father of John Wesley, did infinitely better, for he went up to Oxford with less than three guineas, and so organized things that after he had taken his degree he went away with £10 15s.!

Now, as I think of poor scholars I have known personally who have done notable work, Henry Bradley, who was, as you know, one of the editors of the *Oxford English Dictionary*, and Alfred Williams stand out prominently among them, and I propose not to worry you with a long list of people but to tell you something of Henry Bradley and Alfred Williams. I expect you have not heard the name of Alfred Williams, but you are hearing it now, and that is what is called education!

But I cannot forbear just a glance at three other people. Whenever I think of education I think of Margaret McMillan, who has had more effect on English education than any other person in the last fifty years. She was the mother of medical inspection, followed by treatment, for children, and she founded the first open-air nursery school, which is the highest expression of education I have ever seen. But she started with nothing but her indomitable spirit—literally nothing. She was a person who lived in the spirit and never regarded anything of 'this world' as of any importance. When she wanted a new hat she sent the charwoman out to buy it, and the charwoman, with wisdom which is common among south London ladies, chose one to suit herself, and secured the reversion of it—very rapidly. She had no friends, nothing but her spirit, and she did all that wonderful work. I sometimes think that Margaret McMillan was the greatest person I have ever known.

I turn from her to Reuben George, who had lost his fingers in the course of his work. He was firstly a soap-box orator, 'down with everything that is up,' but he got converted as the result of a visit to Oxford, and at once started to be an apostle of sweetness and light. He built up his library, and literally for years in Swindon, every Saturday in the summer, he led hundreds out to places of historical interest, and every Saturday night in the winter you would find an audience of three or four hundred, even when it was raining hard, all listening to the best lecturers he could get for them. He was not afraid to ask anybody. Such men as Lord Haldane and Robert Bridges lectured regularly. And when Reuben died last year all Swindon turned out and the great parish church of Swindon was packed with people who had come to pay a tribute to this workman who believed in education so much. The good that that man did is incalculable in its effect in inspiring people to study and sending the young people of Swindon on to further education.

And then I think of a young man I met once. He, too, was an extreme politician when I met him. I found out that he had been in blind-alley employment up to the age of

eighteen years.   He began by knocking railway men up in the
morning early; then he was in a cycle yard; in fact, he did any
odd job that came along.   Then he became inspired by a
scrap of science.   There was in the town where he lived a
schoolmaster who didn't say: 'What's the use of your starting
to study?'   He encouraged him, and in a year or two he got
a bursary at the neighbouring university college.   I think it
was about £30 a year.   His father was doing his twelve
hours a day on money that was not more than the dole is now,
and keeping a large family.   But, to cut a long story short, a
real life of learning has made that man one of the greatest
medical researchers of our time.   He did not begin till he
was eighteen.   Then he had, humanly speaking, no chance,
but his indomitable spirit made it.

And now let me come to my two people—Henry Bradley
and Alfred Williams.   I take these two, as I have said,
because I knew them.   I met Henry Bradley when I was a
schoolboy of fourteen years of age, and he was then poor and
ill.   I did not know it at the time, but he had ventured to
London a few years previously after serving twenty years as a
correspondence clerk in a Sheffield firm.   This had closed
down, and he had been one of those who had got what is
euphemistically called 'the sack.'   He supported his family
—five daughters and a son—by the proceeds of literary hack-
work, reviewing books even on cookery and conjuring.   He
developed incomparable scholarship in those Sheffield years
of working from 9 a.m. to 6 p.m.   The chance came to him
to write a review of one of the early issues of the *Oxford English
Dictionary*.   Sir James Murray saw it, recognized the quality
of the man, and determined to have him on his staff.   I
remember, when I went to see him as a boy, he had just been
given an honorary M.A. degree at Oxford, and had been
elected president of the Philological Society.   This charming
man talked to me, a schoolboy, just as he talked to Robert
Bridges thirty years later.   If you want to read a beautiful
piece of English, read Robert Bridges's introduction to the
collected works of Henry Bradley.   He talked to me, as I
have said, in just the same way as Bridges records, and he

expressed just the same kindly delight in simple things. It delighted him to have been addressed on the morning of one of my visits by a Frenchman as 'respectable sir.' Bridges notes his delight in verbal comicalities and unintentional malapropisms. It must have been about that time that he performed the remarkable feat recorded by Robert Bridges. His wife was ill and, like a good many husbands, he was not of much use under those circumstances, but his affection for her made him want to sit in the sick-room. To pass the time he took a plain Russian text and, with no help but an alphabet and his knowledge of the principles of Indo-Germanic philology—at that time he knew no Slavonic languages—in a week he made out one word in three, and at the end of a fortnight had mastered the book. He said that the proper names had helped him to construct a table of inflections. Well, that's pretty thick! I asked a Russian scholar what he thought of it, and he said it might be possible for a genius, and, of course, Bradley was a genius. He was so simple, as great men are, and he enjoyed the common events of life. He even acted as sidesman at a church at Clapham until he found himself involved in a procession up the aisle carrying a palm in his hand, and that was too much for him. But he had impregnable faith in the spiritual governance of mankind, and this was, he believed, determined in him by his brave father's example in having renounced his worldly prospects rather than tamper with his conscience.

Bradley was even more inspiring than his work. An American schoolboy found in meeting him the most remarkable of his experiences in England. 'We have nobody quite like him in America,' he said, and although the boy could not be presumed to know America—who does?—he was probably right, for Bradley was indeed *sui generis*.

In later years I met him at the Oxford Press and in Magdalen College. He became a Fellow of Magdalen at sixty-five or so, and had to wait on young Fellows of twenty-two or twenty-three. He was just the same simple, unaffected man—a great scholar. As Spenser is the poets' poet, so Bradley is the scholars' scholar.

Probably the biggest thing that fell to Bradley was friendship with Bridges. You can imagine the two old cronies talking over everything that happened in the world. I wonder how much of Bradley found its way into *The Testament of Beauty*? But what Bridges said of him at the end is so beautiful that I venture to read it:

He was one of those who, having neither inclination nor temptation to accept the world as it stands, are early driven to live to themselves, and by instinctive self-protection preserve that simplicity and purity of mind which is the foundation of all that is good whether in thought or conduct. In that contemplative detachment from conventional valuations, human sensibility is heightened both in delicacy and emotion by a profounder perception of the ideal significance of Appearance, and the feelings are transported into a spiritual world where accidents of Being are but ephemeral shows. Bradley lived in that ideal world which assured faith in the promises of man's desire, and in a life after death where they would be fulfilled. Though no man could better understand the objections with which material science could forbid such hopes—and he was presumably no better able than another to picture any sort of future existence which should be sufficiently like our present state to continue our mortal sympathies, or, if it should continue them, could continue to satisfy them—yet this agnosticism did not destroy the faith in which Bradley lived and died.

And difficult as it is with our sorrowful experience to face with any comfort the prospect of a general resurrection, yet there is none of us who would not desire to meet his old friends again, and cannot picture the joy of it. I myself would risk a good deal on the chance of meeting Henry Bradley: indeed, all my memories of him are so pleasant that I can almost imagine the delight of his company enduring *in aeternum*.

Bradley received the reward of his scholarship, and I think it is good to look for a few moments at such a man, simple and pure, who had no chance whatsoever in the ordinary expression of the word. Of course, he was a genius, but every man and woman is a genius in some way. It may not come out in college, but that is not to say that they are not so. There is not a man or woman alive who has not some quality which surpasses the common qualities. We are all in some way or other geniuses; we usually fail to get it recognized, however.

Now I come to Alfred Williams. Alfred Williams was the son of a village carpenter at South Marston in Wiltshire. He left school altogether at the age of eleven years. At the age of nine he was doing half-time at school and half-time at his work, pulling thistles out of the ground, scaring birds, and doing anything that an animated boy could do, if he was, so to speak, made to.   At the age of eleven he was able to go into Swindon as a furnace boy in the Great Western Railway works there.   He lived six miles out of Swindon, and he had to work, as indeed he did for twenty years, somewhere about twelve hours a day.   It was some time before he could get anything like a bicycle, and you would see the small boy trudging into Swindon and out of Swindon and working twelve hours a day.   Here is his account of five days out of seven:

I get up at about 5 a.m.   Before leaving for work I do some study in the form of reading, then I cycle into Swindon, where I have to start at 6 a.m. During my meals I work at French and Latin, and at night devote a little time to Greek.   I leave work at 5.30 p.m. and, after doing necessary shopping, cycle home and settle down to literary work until bedtime.

Almost a night-club!   Well, you say, what is the good of an uneducated boy doing that kind of thing?   He had no teachers, mind you.   It was all on his own that he did it, yet in some mysterious way, it was instinct I suppose, he did not try to avoid manual labour because he felt it stimulated his mind and spirit.   He never studied on Sunday, but took his walks and went to church.   It would be incredible, if it were not true, that during these twenty years he wrote books, published poetry, and mastered Greek and French so that he was able to produce translations which commanded the respect of scholars and poets.   How did he do it?   You say: 'Oh, you can tell me!'   But you can go to your library and find there the published works of Alfred Williams.   I will read the list of them to you:

Songs in Wiltshire.
Poems in Wiltshire.
Nature and Other Poems.
Cor Cordium.
War Sonnets and Songs.
Selected Poems.
Folk Songs of the Upper Thames.
Tales of the Panchantantra (translated from the Sanskrit).

And his prose works:

A Wiltshire Village.
Life in a Railway Factory.
Villages of the White Horse.
Round about the Upper Thames.

This record would lead one to suppose him a bookish fellow, but Alfred Williams rejoiced in everything—his simple walks on Sunday, the beauty of the countryside, its flowers and trees, the manners and experiences of his fellow workers.   His books *A Wiltshire Village* and *Villages of the White Horse* make that perfectly clear.   He left the factory after twenty years because his health would not allow him to continue.   But at once he started to scour the country round, cycling more than thirteen thousand miles in order to discover the folk-songs of the Upper Thames.   This is his own story of how he did it:

> The greater part of the work of collecting the songs must be done at night, and winter is the best time, as the men are then free from their labours after tea.   This necessitates some amount of hardship, for one must be prepared to face all kinds of weather, and to go long distances.   Some idea of the amount of travel necessary to the work may be gathered from the fact that in nineteen months I cycled more than thirteen thousand miles.   In frost and snow, fogs, rain, and on sultry summer nights I have journeyed along the dark roads, and climbed the steep hills bordering the valley, with the bats, the owls, the hares, and the foxes.   I have faced the Thames floods in almost inky blackness upon unknown roads and lanes, and shivered in the numbing cold of the damp mists exhaled by the river in the late autumn and winter months.   Once, during a severe flood, following an extraordinarily rapid rise of water, I found myself immersed to the waist, in Stygian darkness, and miles from any town or village; I have often scrambled along the banks in the blackness above the roaring brooks to escape a wetting. In the spring I have loitered on my return, evening after evening, till past midnight, listening to the nightingale under the pure air and clear skies of the Cotswolds.   Later in the summer, at the same hour, I have sat in the grass by the roadside amid the beautiful glow-worms, while the air was warm and fragrant with the delicious scents of the newly made hay.   I have watched the late moon rise, now from behind the Cotswolds, and now above the rolling chalk downs of Berkshire, south of the White Horse; and I have looked upon its reflection at midnight in the calm river, now from Swinford, now from New Bridge or Radcot, and again from the Ha'penny Bridge at Lechlade, or at Castle Eaton.

And, you see, you can get from your library the folk-songs. Six hundred of them are published, and six hundred of them are not published.

You must not think that Alfred Williams looked like 'Bloomsbury.'   If you had not known him you would have thought he was just a farm labourer.   There was nothing, unless you looked into his eyes, to give you any idea that there was anything remarkable in this man.   It is literally true of him that everything that was pure and true was an immediate inspiration to him to serve. In all his writing there is no complaint. Everything was turned by the alchemy of his spirit to good and high use. He was independent, scorned publicity, would not prostitute literary work for money. When he wrote the *Wiltshire Village*—and it was true of the rest—Alfred Williams put down what he saw. The vicar, who did not like it—although he was sorry later—burned the book in a village bonfire, but Alfred Williams would not let that get about because he hated the publicity that—such is our attitude to literature—would have sold thousands of copies. And nothing would he do below the highest that he could possibly do, and throughout his life he never had an income of £2 a week, and for large parts of it less than £1. He never got anything out of his books, though the publishers obviously did.

He was married, and his helpmate must have heen God-given, or he could not have done the work he did.

When he got well enough he tried to go to the war. They wouldn't let him for a long time, but at last he went to India. John Bailey, who was literary critic of *The Times*, has recorded somewhere his general's statement that he was the best gunner in the battery. When out there he learnt Sanskrit, and his translations from the Sanskrit were published at Oxford. This was really astonishing. When he came back from India he went into market gardening. His crops failed, but nobody had any idea that Alfred Williams was really on the edge of starvation, and if anybody had given him any money he would have returned it. An Oxford scholar sent him something to go to a summer school, but it did not suit his proud nature. He told my wife once that his strawberry crop was failing, but we never knew how poor he was, we never knew it at all.

And then, you see, literary work and everything was not enough. He and his wife set to work to build their own house with their own hands. They got something from a subsidy and Lord Fitzmaurice gave them something to help build the house. They went to a disused canal lock where there were stones, and carted them to the house—and a first-class house it is, any building society would advance on it. It is as good a little house as you can find, and they built it with their own hands.

And then came tragedy. His wife fell ill with a dread disease, and he, after cycling down to Swindon to visit her in hospital, passed away, I suppose absolutely worn out. He died from heart failure, just as the Prime Minister granted him a Civil List pension.

You can't understand such a man, can you? But what I am telling you is literally true. I do not think there is any nobler story in the life of modern England. His books will remain as genuine representations of the life of his time as he knew it. No historian in the future can allow himself to miss them. His works on village life stand side by side with his *Life in a Railway Factory*. He spoke the truth as he saw it. He must remain a mystery. Those who knew him have erected two slight memorials, one a tablet on the house he built, and another tablet in the town hall at Swindon, and, then, after his death a small sum of money came to his wife— I think it was £50 the Prime Minister sent—and she devoted it to the erection of a memorial in the churchyard.[1] Lest my story be still deemed incredible, let it be said that Mr. John Bailey, who later wrote an introduction to his selected poems, expressed wonder and astonishment when he wrote of 'this born artist, who, sustained by beauty, early divined in it the key to complete experience, until all adversities of circumstance of which he had so heavy a share fell into their subsidiary place and became transitional.'

> I will sing my song triumphantly,
> I will finish my race,
> I will work my task.

There is an epic of a real workman scholar. I do not know any comparable to him. He wanted nothing except to do his work.

One of my definitions of an educated man is the ability to do without things which are not necessary to complete expression, and to find happiness and joy in the things that cost

---

[1] There are now memorials also on Liddington and Barbary Hills.

nothing—they are the best things. I admit I don't come up to my ideal because I smoke a pipe, but directly I can forget that pipe I shall know that my education is increasing. But there is not much chance of my doing that.

You will say that the life of Alfred Williams ended so sadly. Yes, it did. But in these days of perplexity and change we may take courage from the simple view of such a man. Let us take as symbolical his outlook on the countryside he loved. We should all be able to see the beauty in life, no matter what happens, no matter what comes, and to get that courage which drives out fear. Why should anybody fear? Courage comes from the real, true view of life; fear, even in the most terrible days, is not worthy of a man, is not worthy of an educated man. The right view of life gives courage, courage to face what comes, and Henry Bradley had it, and Alfred Williams had it.

As Williams wrote:

> There 's double harvest in the fields
>   And double on the plain,
> And double-handed plenty yields
>   The double glinting grain;
> There 's sweet wild honey from the bees
>   Where the purling fountains rise,
> And the shady honours of the trees
>   Make a lovely paradise.
> And the hills are always green, my boys,
>   And the hills are always green,
> The high sun shines on the oaks and vines
>   And the hills are always green.

And we can take that as symbolical of the view of life we should all hold.

ACKNOWLEDGMENTS

THANKS are due to those who have permitted the reproduction of the articles and addresses, including:

The Manchester University Press for 'Working Men and Continuation Schools' from *Continuation Schools in England and Elsewhere*, edited by the late Sir Michael Sadler.

The Society for Promoting Christian Knowledge and the Sheldon Press for 'Education and Worship.'

The Rolls House Publishing Company Ltd. and the editor of *The Church Quarterly Review* for 'Church Tutorial Classes.'

The Cambridge University Press for 'Citizenship' from *Cambridge Essays on Education*, edited by the late Mr. A. C. Benson.

The Oxford University Press and the Rt. Hon. Oliver Stanley, M.P., for Chapter I, Part II of *The Way Out*.

Ernest Benn Ltd. for 'The Power of the Spirit' from *The Educated Life* in the 'Affirmation' series.

The Principal and Birkbeck College, University of London, for 'The Dedication of Life,' being the Second Annual Haldane Memorial Lecture delivered at the college.

Victor Gollancz Ltd. for 'The Demands of the Ordinary Man' from *Christianity and the Crisis*, edited by the late Dr. Percy Dearmer.

The Principal and Union Society, Institute of Education, University of London, for the Foundation Oration, 'Some Workman Scholars,' delivered at the institute.

BOOKS BY ALBERT MANSBRIDGE

(Not including numerous booklets)

1913. UNIVERSITY TUTORIAL CLASSES (Longmans).

1920. AN ADVENTURE IN WORKING-CLASS EDUCATION (Longmans).

1923. THE OLDER UNIVERSITIES OF ENGLAND (Longmans).

1932. MARGARET MCMILLAN: PROPHET AND PIONEER (Dent).

1934. BRICK UPON BRICK (Dent).

1935. EDWARD STUART TALBOT AND CHARLES GORE (Dent).

1940. THE TRODDEN ROAD (Dent).